n the /

News:
A N Wilson new president of Morrab Library / Page 25

hman

24 JANUARY 2002

certainty

eorge's
tary

the job of attempting to knock
ch
wl
lig

which an impending crisis is looming. Many of us who had been looking forward to considered debate sat in gloom at the prospect of a pointless battle leading to an unappetising stalemate.

The ritual point scoring across the chamber is deeply unedifying if your concerns provide the matter being used as convenient ammunition to lob across at your opponent.

But at least it takes the Government's eyes off the activities of the Lobby fodder behind them

ni

5 JULY 2001

B**RIEF** N E W S

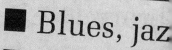

■ Blues, jaz

Impressions of a raw recruit
through selected Parliamentary Sketches and Essays

1997—2002

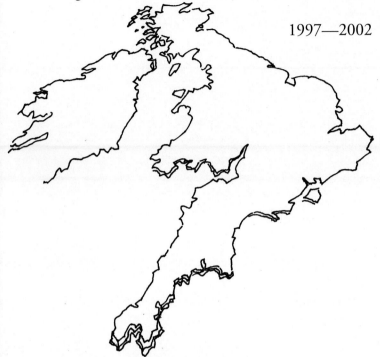

A View from the Bottom Left-Hand Corner

Andrew George MP

WITH ILLUSTRATIONS BY TONY EVERSHED

By the same author:
"Cornwall at the Crossroads" *(with R. Perry and B. Deacon),* 1989,
"The Natives are Revolting down in the Cornwall Theme Park", 1986
and "A Vision of Cornwall" (1993).

Pubished by The Patten Press, 2002
© Andrew George
All rights reserved.
ISBN 1 872229 45X
Printed and bound in Great Britain by Century Litho Company, Penryn,
Falmouth, Cornwall

Gwary wheag ew gwary teag.

(Fair play is beautiful play.)

Cornish motto associated with 'hurling', and adopted by St Ives Rugby Club

Acknowledgements

Though none of those mentioned below share any of the blame for this volume, I would not have achieved even this without the diligent and dedicated support of Ursula Cooper who translated and typed my incoherent scribbles, and to Emma Williams and Judy Anderson, partners in the crime.

Richard Vanhinsberg (Editor) and staff of *The Cornishman* Newspaper deserve special mention for permitting me the freedom to offload the frustrations, joys and musings of a stressed-out Member of Parliament once every two weeks in the popular and well read columns of that newspaper under the banner "Parliamentary Sketch".

Simon Griffiths, Tricia Sanderson, Andy McGuffie and Andy Evans have variously offered more comments (too often overruled by me), research and advice. Also to Melissa Hardie for her support throughout and Lucy Evershed for her indexing and editing.

Tony Evershed has not only turned a text displeasing to the mind into something pleasing to the eye but, like others, he has patiently coaxed me towards textual, grammatical and material improvements. He has also added immeasurably with his pen sketches.

Finally I must thank Paul Flynn, MP for Newport West, whose excellent book, *"Commons Knowledge"* receives many references in this book. I don't doubt that I have shamelessly plagiarised more from it than I have been able fully to acknowledge in the footnotes.

A.G.

Photography: Thanks to Sam Morgan-Moore (cover, pages 73, 79 and 154); Parliamentery Recording Unit (cover, 10, 134); Captain Keith Blount, RN (26, 67); school photo (36); Tony Evershed (55); Peter Lough MP (60); Peter George (103); Cornwall & Isles of Scilly Press (120, 179); Colin MacLaren (173).

CONTENTS

1999-2000

2000–01

2001–02

Each of these essays was written as a "Parliamentary Sketch" for *The Cornishman* Newspaper unless otherwise indicated.

Foreword

by Michael White

THE OTHER DAY a friend sent me an article he'd picked up on a website. It was called *The Killing of Cornwall* and claimed to show that the Treasury in London takes more in taxes out of its poorest county in England than it puts in through grants and other payments.

I know that Tony Blair is aware that Cornwall is the country's poorest county because a Downing Street official, more surprised than I was, informed me of the fact prior to the Prime Minister's flying visit in 2000.

Much good it has done Cornwall so far and my local sources weren't too impressed by his grip on the rural post office problem either. But we live in hope that Mr Blair will prise Gordon Brown's hands off the Treasury cheque book long enough to match the EU funds promised under Objective One—and let the money be spent.

I also know that Andrew George is well aware of the day-to-day implications of such grim statistics because he has hammered away at them since seeing off David Harris, my former fellow political correspondent at Westminster and Conservative MP for St Ives until 1997.

Harris was a gentle kind of MP, not the sort of chap who would say, as one Cornish Tory cheerfully confided during the last row with the Spaniards, that "all fishermen are pirates". Herbivorous by nature he rose to his dizziest heights as unpaid Parliamentary Private Secretary to Sir Geoffrey Howe before Sir G jumped over the cliff, taking Margaret Thatcher (and David) with him.

Andrew George is made of sterner stuff. He has rebelled over the bombing of Iraq, fought for his constituency fishermen, grappled (as David Penhaligon used to do) between his Green instincts and the knowledge that Cornwall needs its cars and cheaper petrol. Older readers remember that Penhaligon's 5p a gallon rural discount was one of the few Liberal gains from the 1997–8 Lib-Lab pact.

Young George is also a trustee of the Rural Race Equality Project which, in his case, must mean protecting the grockles in their summer

1

cottages on the Penwith Peninsula. All in all he has the instincts to become one of that invaluable parliamentary gang, the all-party Awkward Squad.

An endangered species whose honorary president is Tam Dalyell, the Labour Old Etonian, the awkward squad are the trouble-makers, the ones who do not ever want to become junior minister for paper clips.

This collection of parliamentary sketches and essays, mostly written as a regular column for *The Cornishman,* reveals another attractive quality: sceptical and self-deprecating humour, enough to realise (rare for a Liberal Democrat) that the Jenkins Commission on Electoral Reform will never be a best-seller in Halsetown (where my grandfather was born) nor Mullion where Andrew learned his ABC when I was doing A-levels at Bodmin Grammar.

I grew up in Cornwall of mainly Cornish stock. My father was a master mariner, born in St Just (the other St Just he would explain, not smart St Just In Roseland) and his father a tin miner. They both travelled the world, but came home to live—and die. I and my brothers and sisters, most of our Cornish cousins too, have also left and may not come back except for our annual Easter gathering in St Ives—where our parents first met. Last year, now three generations again, there were 26 of us.

That helps to put a few bob in the till at The Sloop and the Balancing Eel chip shop next door. But that will not be enough to turn Cornwall around. Nor will the Tate of the West, the new university, nor the brilliant Eden Project outside St Austell where I lived until I was 11. No, after the thumping Cornwall and its industries have suffered for years, it will need much more concerted help from outside, which means from governments in London and even the dreaded Brussels.

Meanwhile I am grateful to Andrew George's collection for telling me that responsibility for the Cornish language once lay with the Welsh Office and not the Department of Culture (odd that) and for honouring that vital Cornish word for procrastination, as in "I'll do it dreckly". Let's hope prosperity rolls in a bit more dreckly than usual.

Political Editor, *The Guardian*

INTRODUCTION

AFTER FINDING myself catapulted into the House of Commons, I had no intention of commencing a political career by writing a book about it. It has all happened by accident.

As a politician, I would like to think this volume will be anxiously sought by an adoring public, but I suspect it will be studied by a few anthropologists seeking revealing evidence of how a comprehensively challenged and self-confessed unreformable bumpkin made his way in the refined culture of London and the Palace of Westminster.

I am well aware that in publishing this book I am entering "clever dick" territory. But the purpose is to present a document which charts some of the reflections of a relatively new Member of Parliament facing the demands, pressures and opportunities of taking on one of the most challenging and geographically remote constituencies in the country.

But whilst I come from one of the most exceptional parts of the country I in fact write as an unexceptional, regular homo sapiens, a run-of-the-mill kind of chappie; which are unusual qualities to find amongst the super human beings generally found in the upper echelons of politics.

Perhaps it is my lack of having a "mainstream" political background and pedigree that has made me unimpressed by those who seek the pursuit of politics as a dedicated evangelising of their own political dogma.

My own dogma is simply a "make it up as I go along" approach, with all of its inevitable inconsistencies. (A politician who isn't inconsistent should never be trusted.)

By and large, two themes run through the book. The first is the teasing out of the gap between the real world and the political discourse in Westminster. I often reflect as I travel from the far West of Cornwall to London on the eons of intergalactic space between the House of Commons and the real world. Westminster has many redeeming features, but a reflection of reality is generally not one of them.

Secondly, is the uneasy relationship between politics and the media.

Because all politicians desperately want to appear popular and relevant at all times, we are people who by circumstance and condition are often neurotically obsessed with our own self publicity.

At worst, politicians will bask in other people's glory or brazenly make public capital out of other people's private tragedies. The contemporary anxiety to sprint from the Commons down to waiting journalists to get "on the record" comment before even your political colleagues brings out all of the worst in human nature and demonstrates, to the media at least, why politicians are generally and universally loathed.

I came into politics after an immediate previous life of being a charity worker. I know it seems improbable. In the generally understood league tables in which the public view the esteem of various professions and callings, charity workers are up there at the top of the premiership division competing with Archangels, Richard Branson, Bob Geldof and so on, whereas politicians are found grubbing around towards the bottom of the lowest division, competing with intrusive tabloid journalists, the paparazzi, estate agents (except, of course, those living in the St Ives constituency), nuisance neighbours and Beelzebub himself.

Why did I do it? I hear you ask. I still haven't found an answer.

But those involved in the media certainly have a clear view of who falls lower down the ratings than the other. I am sure that Robert Harris of *The Telegraph* was writing on behalf of many columnists when he claimed that people who are first rate "head towards the media leaving politics… to the second-rate."[1]

The choice is simple. "Which would you rather be—the hunter or the hunted?"[2] "Would you rather have much more money, never be held to account when you get things wrong, and enjoy an unscrutinised private life? Or would you rather toil in obscurity, in the vague hope of one day being responsible for Railtrack or the NHS, while having every aspect of your finances and sexuality picked over, before being dumped by the electorate? Tough choice eh?"[1]

I suppose it's nice to have a hint of sympathy from our tormentors in the media and I do hope that this rather more candid portrayal of an early life on the backbenches will serve some interest to those who follow public and political life, even if it doesn't contribute anything more than most of the rest of politics to the sum of human knowledge or general happiness!

West Cornwall 2002

[1]   *Why would anyone want to be a poor politician? Robert Harris, The Daily Telegraph, Tuesday 11th December 2001*
[2]   *Attrib. Max Hastings, Editor of The Evening Standard, 11th December 2001*

Successful year for the downwardly mobile

THE CORNISH have always had a cunning method of dealing with the prospect of ignominy; the early use of the noble art of self-depreciation.

For many, like me, it is a chronic and untreatable condition brought on by centuries of deference to the Saxons since King Athelstan drew a line at the River Tamar between England and Cornwall in 936, when he concluded the Cornish weren't worth the effort of inevitable annihilation.

It was, therefore, natural that my first year's Parliamentary goal should be to establish myself firmly as the 659th most effective MP in the Commons Chamber.

And, before my waggish colleagues advise that I shouldn't set my sights too high, it should be understood that my ingenious master plan was to ensure that, once achieved, I had nowhere else to go but up.

What I hadn't reckoned upon was that, instead of it taking a very special effort on my part, it would all come so naturally.

Many honourable colleagues cancel appointments to enjoy the customary lengthy interventions and admonitions from Madam Speaker whenever the Member for St Ives rises to stumble his way through another oral question; or entertains connoisseurs of the select committee by successfully being skewered into a corner by witnesses who, until they met me, were on the verge of throwing in the towel.

Panic did set in once when a broadsheet Parliamentary sketch writer—obviously short of good copy—disappointed with a column describing one of my Chamber offerings as "Speech of the Week". Fortunately, closer inspection suggested that it may have been the subject rather than the oratorial craft which generated the accolade.

Just in case any lasting damage had been done to my reputation, I had to put the matter in balance, and quickly achieved this when, having misinterpreted advice, I droned on for far too long in a later debate; an achievement which prompted the Member for Greenock and Inverclyde to honour me with a very personal rendition of a choice selection from his probably slim volume of gratuitous unparliamentary language.

Whilst, sadly for the Cornish, I am the living embodiment of some of the worst racist stereotypes they too often have to endure, the truth is that they are just like any other members of the human race—bright, able, and, given the opportunity, capable of great success. Unfortunately, most of them are rarely given the opportunity or resources but become resigned to their lot as quaint, deferential appendages to a beautiful landscape or a holiday experience—for which they are envied and their poverty ignored.

However, a year on—so I theorised—it was time to mastermind my way up from last place, and was soon heartened by a generous invitation to a select dinner to discuss the great affairs of state with the great and good. Bursting to tell everyone, I immediately showed the invitation to my esteemed colleague and mentor Jackie Ballard, anticipating that she would look on me in a new light—a worthy entrant to the select band of thrusting, upwardly-mobile MPs destined for stardom.

But she puffed: "Oh I had my invitation weeks ago!" and handed it back to a small heap of crestfallen, humbled backbench lobby fodder. Desolate, I crept out into the mist-wreathed wastes of Westminster…

…Meanwhile, six hours' journey away from the theatre of the Commons, the reality of the coal-face of my constituency beckons, where a small but happy band of staff assist in securing modest but real achievements against the daily tidal wave of constituents' casework.

Written for 'The House' Magazine, July 20th 1998

Recycling politicians

COMMON perception suggests that our MPs make England football supporters look like models of decorum and decency; and (with, of course, the honourable exception of the Member for St Ives) this may be true.

This week our behaviour was put to the test. We were permitted out of the heavily cordoned secure unit we're kept in for most of the week—known to most people as the Palace of Westminster—to take part in the early morning Parliamentary Bike Ride from Covent Garden back to the custody of the Commons. The foolhardy heroes arranging the event were the officers of the All Party Parliamentary Cycling Group who all come from various cycling campaign societies and clubs.

The event gives those MPs who are desperate to demonstrate their cycling credibility a chance to show it, and cycling lobby groups a golden opportunity cynically to skewer innocent MPs on the public record while offering them a cold croissant, coffee and a photo opportunity.

Just like last year, I was keen to show my support. It was for a distance of only about 2 miles (and a gentle downhiller at that) and would finish in plenty of time before my first (Select Committee) meeting of the day.

So, after trying to do too much as usual in the office beforehand, I arrived concerned that I may be late. But I needn't have worried. The interminable photo shoots were still in full swing. The problem was that there were too many MPs even for the multitude of wide-angle lenses.

It was not a pretty sight. Serried ranks of earnest looking Lib Dems in helmets and clips, a couple of immaculate Tories who would have looked better on penny farthings than on mountain bikes and a happy bunch of New Labour MPs who had swapped the cloth cap for lycra shorts and, if you believe some of the press, only one "thinly disguised" Cornish nationalist! Even the Deputy Sergeant-at-Arms had replaced his sword and garter for bike and helmet.

The challenge for the organisers was somehow to get this convoy of jostling egos down to the Commons without causing a by-election.

Nervous marshals, guiding us through the death wish traffic mecca of Trafalgar Square, politely reminded us it was "not a race". But some of the more thrusting MPs amongst us knew that the first into New Palace Yard could take "pole position" in the photo shoot afterwards.

Early arrivals were followed by others who clearly hadn't seen a bike since distant childhood, but we were all grateful for their support nonetheless.

After we had all come panting into the security of the Commons we were into another photo shoot. And, dear constituents, I hope you will understand that when it comes to the unseemly scramble for attention on occasions like this, your representative prefers to stand back and watch from a respectful distance.

Whilst I am sure that the campaign groups will be happy that the interests of cycling were served by this kind of event, it is also certain that the requirement for national security was only restored after all of the MPs were safely goaded back into their lair.

18th June 1998

Commons' yobbery steals the Oscars again

"**WHAT YOU** have to remember, Andrew," advised a senior and respected colleague in the Commons' Tea Room after a particularly torrid parliamentary session, "is that the Commons Chamber is a stage. You are performing, not debating."

His advice had already come too late. I was probably still visibly shaken from a joint lynching during Welsh questions and I kept reassuring myself I would learn the lesson this time. Now, the world hadn't come to an end but I had failed to capitalise fully on an opportunity.

Because, what ardent Commons watchers will know, and I am still learning, is that the craft of politics is more important than the substance.

In a brief opportunity to exchange a few questions on Welsh matters I had one for the Secretary of State on his Country's connection with Cornwall.[1] Not many people will be aware, for example, that responsibility for the development of the Cornish language now falls to the Welsh Office and not to the Department of Culture.

My two-part question would be brief and seek to secure his attention to this important relationship.

However, the problem I hadn't prepared myself for was that the Chamber was rapidly filling with a majority of MPs who had no interest in Welsh questions, even less Cornish ones to the Welsh Secretary as they claimed their seats for Prime Minister's Questions (PMQs) time only a few minutes later. I had also failed to appreciate the effect of a good lunch on the spirits of the Tory backbenchers congregating nearby.

I had observed Commons rowdyism before, but never experienced it. The weapons deployed to destroy the composure of an MP are many and various.

GENERATING sheer volume across the Chamber usually has little impact because the effect is dissipated by the distance. A more subtle but effective method is to use body language. To synchronise the whole of an opposite bench into carefully choreographed body language rejection contortions can sap confidence and lower the temperature of a question or remark. Reading the finale of a carefully prepared edge-of-seat question, only to look up to a sea of faces buried in intent mutual conversations with each other can kill off the punch line of even the most experienced member.

The other, occasionally used method of "chirping" has proven to be effective with some. A member for a South Devon seat—whose past includes a brush with the Law and a taxi firm over an alleged drink-driving offence—is invariably greeted to his feet with the call "Taxi" from opposite benches. Though he soldiers on, a chamber vibrating with uncontrollable laughter is infertile ground for serious consideration.

BUT now, within a few minutes of PMQs my question was about to be called. The first tabled question was answered with helpful acknowledgments and support.

I rose to my feet for my "supplementary". The chamber full. "Does the Secretary of State agree with me…"

A successful start, I thought. The Secretary of State was already listening closely and nodding agreement.

But, of course, the Tory benchers had already decided they were opposed and began to generate a wall of noise between me and the

benches opposite.

Noise from opposite benches can usually be dealt with. In some cases you can use it to spur you on, but organised yobbery between opposition benches can be devastating.

I was still puncturing this wall of sound and was reaching my finale when "Order, Order" rang out. I sat, relieved that at last Madam Speaker had come to my rescue.

Only a few feet away, I glanced across at my tormentors. How I would relish this moment! Except that, when it came, our Betty took exception to me and wanted "the honourable member to put his question".

Unable to protest I rose to punch out the handful of missing words through a renewed barrage of noise.

I hardly noticed the very supportive and helpful reply from the Secretary of State. The mood of the House was anxiously anticipating the "gladiatorial" clash of PMQs and uninterested in the delightful detail of Cornish questions.

I SOON RESUMED my composure when I dealt with an urgent constituency problem. The self-importance of members in the Chamber can soon be put in perspective when contrasted with the real problems of real people in the real world.

There were no fatalities in the Chamber that afternoon. But yobbery had stolen the Oscars again and I would have to come back to bid for my Equity card.

30th June 1998

[1] "Celtic Heritage", House of Commons Hansard Oral Answers, 24th June 1998, col. 1036

The great Chief Whip leaves us with a Thought for the Day

IF FRIEDRICH Nietzsche had been right and God really was dead, then "He would have turned in his grave", I thought to myself…

The occasion was a TV news item quite a few years ago reporting an appalling passenger air plane crash in South America. The report cut to a young back-packing and rather wide-eyed and breathless would-have-been passenger of the fated plane who, we were told, missed the flight by ten minutes. And then "the quote":

Smiling—admittedly, I imagine, more from relief than joy—after being prodded by his interviewer he said, "Well, that proves there really must be a God."

If you ascribe to literal translation and believe that God had spared him from going down with the other 250 souls, it obviously wasn't for his thoughtful and selfless diplomacy. But I was sure that God would have been far too busy on the South American mountainside helping the rescue teams, to have had time to slouch in an armchair watching this.

This wasn't a case of "strong words softly spoken", but an earth shattering comment uttered naïvely.

SOME RECENT parliamentary occasions have, in my view, cruelly exposed those of our undignified breed who would claim to have God on their side.

Mainly, these events are when we are left with a "free vote" on a matter of "conscience".

In normal circumstances, the lazy MP can simply follow the shepherding of his/her Party Whip and find out what they have voted for some time afterwards—if ever at all.

The term "Whip" refers to the hunting field where whips are used to goad dim animals to do their master's bidding (though I just can't for the life of me see what the parallel is—but there we are!).

It seems to be essential that Government Whips (of whichever Party) present the symptoms of a naturalised or Party-induced lobotomy. In and around the Chamber, the Government Whips are mute, but omnipresent. Imagination, personality and creativity are viewed with suspicion and when they fix the eye of their victim it is always with the same motionless, dead pan, unflinchingly homicidal look.

But on free votes, MPs who enjoy the comfort and re-assurance of a Whip's "encouragement" and "advice", or who dare not conjure independent thought without authority, usually find themselves rudderless and cast adrift in a sea of conflicting signals and, on many occasions, unable to decide for themselves.

IT IS OFTEN on these occasions that some wheel into the chamber their own effigy of "God as temporary Chief Whip". Usually these self appointed spokesmen (usually it's men) offer a safe harbour for those who fear drowning. Whatever the "moral" issue may be, these confident authorities of the Chief-Whip-from-above will quote selectively from his latest Manifesto—usually, the Bible.

But problems arise—as they often do—when the self-same Chief Whip is then unveiled by authorities on the other side of the argument. The vulnerable are mercilessly left to flounder. How can they choose?

Is the Chief Whip really "loving" or is he "displeased"? Is this a matter on which he is "forgiving" or is he vengeful and intolerant as he sits in "judgement"?

Any self-respecting MP has only to look at their own public image. Most people, hearing that a politician was coming their way, would do the natural thing—hide their children, safely lock away young maidens and household pets, etc., hide all savings under the mattress, keep them on the doorstep and strike up a sceptical pose.

I'm sure God has the same view. And, looking at the deeply fallen specimens of human kind in the House of Commons Chamber, I'm sure he'd rather be seen dead than take sides in a debate on a "free vote".

20th July 1998

End of term relief at the Commons

THE UNMISTAKEABLE signs of the end of a school term were apparent once again in the Commons last week.

Headteacher Blair had pronounced on his end-of-term report and reshuffled his staff [1]; decorators had already prepared many of the corridors for work over the recess; and the children of the chamber stretched the patience of everyone with boisterous over-exuberance.

But, whilst those Ministers who survived the phone-call-waiting were no doubt dreaming of their Tuscan villas, the diligent MP was already preparing to use August to catch up on all of those promised meetings and enquiries.

I remember very well last August, when dealing with the daily tidal wave of casework and meetings, I tried hard to smile benignly whenever I was asked how I was "enjoying (my) holiday".

However, I have to admit that working largely from one base rather than two is good for sanity.

Parliament may not be sitting again until mid-October, but unless you happen to live in a constituency where everyone is wealthy and makes a rapid and long exodus at the beginning of August, or where all constituents are docile, contented and undemanding, the pressures remain.

JUST BEFORE we did break up, I partook in one of the many under-stated successes of the Parliamentary system—the Select Committee.

The Agriculture Select Committee of which I am a member is 11 strong (1 Liberal Democrat, 3 Conservative and 7 Labour). Amongst a number of recent enquiries, we had published a report into the toxicity of a health food supplement know as Vitamin B6.[2]

It became a matter for the Ministry of Agriculture, Fisheries and Food (MAFF) because dietary supplements are considered to be foods rather than medicines (which would otherwise be the province of the Department of Health).

I must admit that before I got involved in the enquiry I didn't know much about this vitamin. Vitamin B6 is the generic term for six closely related chemicals, and is consumed regularly by over 3 million people in this country—either as part of a multi-vitamin intake or on its own.

Consumer concerns about toxic poisoning expressed some years ago generated government assessments which eventually resulted in new draft regulations in April this year proposing to restrict dietary doses of Vitamin B6 to no more than 10 mg per day and to add health warnings to packages.

Unlike the chamber of the Commons—where too high a dose of theatre rather than debate can cause stodginess of the mind—there are still a few places where party attire can be left in the cloakroom and the seeking of unvarnished truth shines through the proceedings. For on this occasion the Select Committee came to pretty well unanimous and cross-party support for a Government review of the science supporting its decision and a raising of the daily limit to at least 100 mg.

The day before recess the government's response was to accept the need for a review of the decision and to defer any legislation until an expert panel had looked at the evidence [3]. In its own quiet and efficient way the Select Committee had produced results where no amount of dispatch box "tub thumping" and theatrical chamber sound-bites would have produced one dent in the armoury of Ministerial resolve.

4th August 1998

[1] At the end of July 1998 Tony Blair completed a Cabinet reshuffle—sacking four Ministers (Harriet Harman, Gavin Strang, David Clark and Lord Richard) and appointing Jack Cunningham as "Cabinet enforcer". Those coming into the Cabinet were Peter Mandelson, Nick Brown, Stephen Byers and Baroness Jay.
[2] 5th Report of the Agriculture Select Committee, Session 97/98, Vitamin B6, 23rd June 1998.
[3] Nick Brown, then Agriculture Minister, responded to the finding of the Committee in the Commons on 30th July 1998.

"People power" completes Cornish Motto

IF AUGUST IS THE MONTH of travel—albeit in an odd "herd instinct" kind of way—then it is also time to scrutinise "modern myths" about it.

That "travel broadens the mind" is a good one. Probably everyone has heard it said so often that they assume it must be true.

Now, Cornwall sees a lot of people come and a lot of people go and, of course, many Cornish people travel. The history of Cornwall over at least the last 100 years is one of many thousands of Cornish folk facing enforced emigration as traditional industries declined. Indeed, Cornish history has created a community more cosmopolitan than many realise.

Some of the most ardent proponents of the "travel broadens the mind" school—either as a way of justifying the expense or disproportionate use of non-renewables—seem to go away with monotonous regularity, travel all over the place and then come back with the same teeny-weeny little mind they went off with in the first place.

Sometimes their minds end up being even teenier as they come back with ever more outrageous views about the "natives" of places visited.

No. Travel doesn't broaden the mind, but if you start with a broad mind there is an enormous amount to be gained from travelling.

THOSE WHO travelled to Cornwall last week may have wondered what all the fuss was about when the Health Secretary arrived, by train, appropriately enough, to be met by a small welcoming party.[1]

For me, the occasion was significant enough—although a long time in coming. Because it marked a turning point in Cornwall's fortunes. "People power" had succeeded where the rantings and pontifications of politicians on their own would have failed.

Frank Dobson—the Secretary of State—had come to Cornwall to explain that he had bowed to public pressure to reject some of the plans of his Government's appointees to close four hospitals and to downgrade other health services. Cornwall had become so used to protesting and complaining with hardly any effect whatsoever that to score such a significant victory has created a shockwave, but encouraged many communities to have a profoundly new sense of confidence in what Cornwall can achieve in the future.

Although I spoke at more rallies, joined more marches, met with more

Ministers more often, asked more questions of the Prime Minister, presented more petitions and answered more letters on this subject than on any other since I was elected—without the many thousands of people who put their heart and soul into the campaign to protect local health services, I would have (as politicians too often do) "become as a sounding brass or a clanging cymbal" *(Cor. 13.1).*

But simply acting as a channel for the message and a mouthpiece for the passion and determination of so many people made my job the easiest of all. I take absolutely no credit at all for the outcome. The credit is entirely due to every single person (and that must be the vast majority of local people) who contributed, even in a small way, to turning what would otherwise have been a rearguard reaction into an immense campaign which demonstrated that with self-belief "people power" can succeed.

Of course, we must still join battle with the decision to transfer children's surgery from the Rainbow Ward and the review of 24-hour casualty cover at West Cornwall Hospital, but across Cornwall as a whole a significant victory was gained.

THE FIRST word of the Cornish motto ("One and All") is always acknowledged to ring true. Sturdy independence and individuality are recognised as the norm in the Cornish character. But now it is clear that Cornwall can only be effective if the motto as a whole can ring true. A strong independent character is one thing, but bringing people together so that the whole adds up to more than the sum of the parts will make Cornish popular campaigns unstoppable.

With "One and All", we can secure the highest level of European grant aid—Objective One; with the support of "One and All" we can face up to the demanding challenges which lie ahead—taking us out of poverty and decline without turning our communities and our environment into a replica of everywhere else; with the support of "One and All" Cornwall can look forward to its future with greater confidence.

We don't have to travel the world to learn this lesson—it is one we have learnt at home.

18th August 1998

[1]   *Frank Dobson visited the constituency on 13th August 1998 to announce the reversal of the Health Authority's proposed closure of four cottage hospitals and down grading of some hospital services. The proposal had generated a vociferous campaign in opposition over the previous 9 months.*

Slowing down to the pace of life in the fast lane

A NOT UNUSUAL thing happened to me this week. A visitor speaking to Bert Pascoe (not his real name) a mechanic, on the forecourt of a local garage—after having his recently expired vehicle brought back to road-worthiness with courteous efficiency—dropped the idle comment into conversation that "You are so lucky down here. The pace of life is so slow."

I watched with interest the pained but patient expression on Bert's face and his struggled attempt to smile as he brought the conversation to a polite close.

How often this scene must be repeated.

Now, I know Bert well, and when he goes up country (or "up to England" as he prefers it) for new equipment induction or refresher courses he is notorious for having got the job done, dusted and polished the car whilst the rest of them are still reaching for their tool boxes.

When he gets home after a long day's work he gets his tool kit out again in the evening and at weekends to make up his salary which is less than half of that earned by less qualified and experienced mechanics in other part of the country. His wife works shift work. His sons and daughters do any work they can lay their hands on and, like most Cornish households, they never seem to "hang around" and rarely get time to be together as a family.

THIS WEEK, Comrade Tone has called the troops back to Parliament to push through what has been publicly described as "anti-terrorist" legislation. Contrary to popular belief, this is not just an unexpected opportunity for MPs to display and compare their suntans. Usually, by the time we get back in October, after weeks in the natural-light-free zone of conference auditoria and smoke filled rooms of fringe meetings, MPs arrive looking haggard and jaded and in need of a summer recess.

It will also be an opportunity to remind myself that if you want anything done in London you can't rouse anyone till 10.00 am at the earliest and the day starts to slide away from about 5.00 pm. Up there I arrive in my office bright and breezy by about 8.00 am (providing the previous night's voting hasn't gone into the wee small hours) and have learnt that it is the exception rather than the rule that you can achieve much from other offices before the time that I am ready for morning "crowst".[1]

Don't get me wrong. London is a wonderful place and there is little doubt there are more talented people per square mile in the capital than in most other places in these islands. Although that is probably because there are more people per square mile than in most other places, the fact is that the sheer volume of people in a place like this with so much money to support the economy, a great deal can be achieved in little time.

However, I have found that rushing around looking very important and frantically busy has become a metropolitan custom—even a disguise for some. In fact, getting some things done can take a tediously long time. Whilst distances are short, you can often select the traffic jam to suit your mood. And, typically, a friend has been waiting for a workman to return to his flat to finish a job started over three months ago. This is a universal rather than geographical problem for people wanting to get things done the world over.

IT IS ODD how people come to these broadbrush generalisations. Once a statement gains common currency people can tend to repeat what they hear without question. That the "pace of life is slow" in Cornwall, has become an unquestioned statement of truth just as "Cornishmen do it dreckly" can be seen on the back window of pretty well every other vehicle around these parts.

One local wag once said that the word "dreckly" was "similar to the Spanish word 'mañana' but without the same sense of urgency"! Stereotypes can become part of a healthy humour—especially if we are able to mock ourselves.

The fact is that the pace of life in Cornwall is pleasantly very slow indeed if you are retired, if you have come down here to retire or to semi-retire or if you are on holiday. But if you are in work or raising a family the pace of life is fast—no slower or faster than anywhere else I would imagine. Although many claim that in order to be in work and to stay in work in Cornwall you can't afford to slow down.

1st September 1998

[1]   Cornish "tea break"

Watch out, the thought police are coming for you

I WAS roughed over again by the Thought Police recently. On this occasion it was from the P.C. (Politically Correct) "-ist" Brigade, as I know them.

For them, if any word can have "-ist" tacked on to it then it becomes an "-ism" which it is their responsibility to challenge.

To them, all "cock ups" are unquestionably conspiracies; everyone else's motives are, without doubt, dubious and impure; and every "slip of the tongue" is deeply revealing—as they alone are the only true protectors of truth and justice.

Personally, I don't envy them. Because they can never afford to be off duty. Politics, of course, is full of them. But they don't accept just anyone into their ranks.

They are those perfect people who are, of course, without sin and whose calling it is to wander the globe pointing out the imperfections in others—no matter how spurious the basis of the charge, no matter how thin the evidence, and irrespective of the need for unfettered debate on the subject.

THOUGH high summer seems to have succumbed to deep winter in a matter of just a week, it is always without fail that on June 22nd every year, I wait for a pregnant pause in any conversation with friends and neighbours to begin shaking my head vigorously, and sucking in air loudly before blowing it out to pronounce: "evenings are pullin' in again, yo".

But this little bit of humour (as I intend it) is, of course, "season-ist" and is offensive to those sensitive about the longevity of summer.

I dread to think how humourless the planet would be if the Thought Police had complete control.

Though if the proverbial Man from Mars dropped in now on the proverbial Man on the Clapham Omnibus he might come to the conclusion that earthlings had lost their sense of proportion.

JUST A YEAR after a world in mourning and remorse promised to learn the lessons from a nosy interest in the private lives of the famous—when Princess Diana and others met an untimely end

20

arguably as a result of that zealous interest—now the most powerful nation on earth has spent over \$50 million and spawned a billion dollar industry by giving nosy parker journalism a new lease of life.[1]

We are assured that it is not about sex—even though it seems to have created a new source of Internet pornography. No. It's about whether the President lied about his private life.

Presumably he might just as well have falsely denied ever having cornflakes for breakfast. But no. That's not the same thing. Because that's not interesting.

Meanwhile, the evening television news—dominated by graphic details and analysis from Washington—is about to come to an end. Usually, immediately before the "and finally" story about dancing guinea pigs in Pickering or whistling dogs in Doncaster, we are shown a brief excerpt from Sudan where thousands of innocent children are dying of starvation. Perhaps the Man from Mars is right to be shocked.

But in this constituency I can confirm that I continue to receive stacks of letters and calls about the problems of under-developed countries and have not received one about the US President. Are we the only place on the planet to have retained our critical faculties, our sanity and our sense of proportion?

14th September 1998

[1] *This was the week that independent Counsel Kenneth Starr told the US Congress there were grounds for impeaching President Bill Clinton because of his attempt to conceal his affair with Monica Lewinsky.*

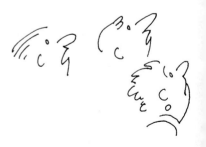

South coast town hit by conference[1]—few survivors

THOSE OF A nervous disposition and those at least moderately sane are always strongly recommended to avoid any English seaside resort beginning with the letter "B" at this time of year.

Because this is the season when Britain's small band of self-confessed political junkies decamp to their Party Conference at Brighton (Liberal Democrats), Blackpool (Labour) and Bournemouth (Tories). I did my penance at Brighton last week.

If (according to Harold Wilson) a week is a long time in politics then it's an eternity of perpetual torment at the Party Conference.

Hotel and Guest House proprietors brace themselves for the onslaught. For them it must be like being invaded by a strange cult of born-again evangelists from hell. Their simple aim is to avoid getting pinned against the wall in conversation over anything other than the "politics free zone" of the weather or directions around town.

For those who like to "surf" hands free around the Conference circuit there's the choice of a week of carefully stage-managed standing ovations (at Bournemouth), a week when "class warriors" are held at bay by "control freaks" (at Blackpool) or there is the annual blood sport of giving the Party leadership a bloody nose to demonstrate party democracy (at Brighton).

Around the Conference auditorium itself is "the Fringe"—hundreds of stalls and meetings which have become increasingly populated with multinational companies which are either without or in desperate need of political friends because they have either wrecked the planet, exploited the poor or done both and have come to display their sudden and complete remorse.

I CAN remember having to save up for decades before I could afford to attend my first Conference (no wonder so few from this area go to them). And apart from a distinct impression that I wanted my money back, I came away with large boxes of leaflets, brochures and (it being the Liberal Democrats) lorry loads of policies which collectively commandeered a whole room in my house!

But, I have to say, for all of their many faults, Party Conferences do have some redeeming features. Because in a world of political tribalism, a strange thing generally happens at Party Conferences.

We all find ourselves having to use the strengths of our arguments and having to listen to the points of view of others, rather than—as politicians famously do all too often—resort to personal attacks or appealing to political loyalty. At our conference I felt compelled to come to the rostrum to respond to the argument of another delegate. I, of course, congratulated him on the strength of his arguments and the quality of his speech. I found many key points on which we agreed but "regretted" the fact that we "came to different conclusions".

Of course, I couldn't attack his appearance, or taunt him about an unfortunate brush with a tabloid newspaper or rubbish the record of the Party he represented—which are some of the conventional rhetorical devices used across the chamber in the House of Commons. Each of those options was closed to me.

The frustrating thing is that a gracious contortion at the rostrum will not give you the tub thumping sound bite needed to dominate all channels of the evening news. A carefully crafted masterpiece may be forever applauded by the Conference anorak but it will remain in the encyclopaedia of anonymity.

In the meantime, the national media assured all Liberal Democrat MPs that there wasn't so much a debate at our Conference as a plot to mount a leadership challenge. The only plot I saw was the plan hatched by some to cleverly use the story for their own self publicity.

However, by the end of the week the world had heard that the "Fatwa" had been lifted. Paddy could sleep soundly in his bed at last...at least until we all return to Brighton again next year.

28th September 1998

[1]   *During this week there was widespread hysteria on the South East Coast of the U.S and great international media anticipation of Hurricane George which was due to hit U.S. states bordering the Gulf of Mexico.*

23

Defending to the death our right to say it

WELL, NOW, Conference season is over. We've all girded our loins; sent the troops back to their constituencies with fire in their bellies and alcoholic residues in their livers; and prepared for the forthcoming Parliamentary year of gladiatorial battles—which begins next week.

Following the Conservatives' conference in Bournemouth last week reminds me how strongly I am opposed to any Fatwa against free speech. As Voltaire said, "I disapprove of what you say, but I will defend to the death your right to say it".[1]

If politicians are confident about their own position then, if they are also honest (a rare combination I know, but let's carry on stretching credulity for a little longer…) there is nothing more motivating than closely following the party conference of your political opposite.

I remember, with some fondness, during the dark days of the "dog eat dog" political culture of the eighties, sharpening my own arguments in response to the carefully orchestrated propaganda stream coming from the party conference of the then government.

IN NORMAL peacetime, political opposition can, in fact, become a deeply unpatriotic business of quietly praying for the worst, secretly shaping the waxed effigies of government aspirations and wishing ill on everything it does.

Fairly scant attention to the most successful post-war opposition party campaigns clearly shows that they have not been about capturing the imagination of the electorate with the sheer brilliance of political ideas, but their ability to seize the opportunity, to feed like successful vultures on the spoils of the political misfortune or mismanagement of the other side.

After a while this becomes an uncomfortably easy part of political instinct—fanning the flames of the doomsday scenario, associating yourself with the collective hand-wringing over the failure of government policy. It's the pastime of the politically talentless, though every politician in opposition has to do the apprenticeship at some time.

Attempting to turn the position of opposition away from opposing the government purely for the sake of it to the promotion of your own preferred policy is challenging—too challenging for some. We, the Liberal Democrats, of course, claim to be the breeding ground for decent political ideas which are often unceremoniously nicked by other parties.

AT PRESENT, for the Conservatives it is much more difficult. It would be easy to gloat at their attempt to avoid their Conference being seen as a parade of losers seeking political relevance. After nearly a complete generation of almost absolute power, it has dawned on keen conference watchers that nothing the Conservatives say matters any longer.

They inevitably have to go through the process of renewing, refreshing and reinventing themselves, just as the Liberal Democrats did after the '87 General Election.

In response to the Labour Party's preaching about the "Third Way" the Conservatives have now come up with their very own "British Way"[2]—though in fact it isn't their very own, it was a major element of a high profile speech given by the Chancellor of the Exchequer (Gordon Brown) as recently as November last year.

Of course, the "Third Way" is well understood by all and can be clearly defined as…well, "something that is not this thing or something else". I hope you are all clear about it now.

I listened to what was meant by the "British Way" in a speech from William Hague and conjured up a distinct image of being invited to jump aboard a rudderless hulk captained by a skipper with blinkers which was destined to founder on rocks as far away from the continent and the real world of multinational economics as humanly possible.

I know that we are all going to have a tremendous amount of fun grappling with these various "Ways" in the House of Commons chamber in the months ahead! I can already feel myself putting some flesh on the bones of a new "Cornish Way" which will be revealed to honourable colleagues in due course.

LAST WEEK'S *Cornishman* report of a Scillonian Councillor defending himself from accusations of behaviour "likely to cause a breach of the peace" in the Islands' Council Chamber sounded tame in comparison with the multiple breaches of peace in the Chamber of the Commons every day.

Personally, I oppose the Fatwa against free speech of people with opposing ideas. I need them to help define and clarify my own views.

13th October 1998

[1]   Attributed to François-Marie Arouet (known as Voltaire) 1694-1778 in S.G. Tallentyre "The Friends of Voltaire" 1907
[2] In his conference speech in October 1998 Hague said: "Our way is not the first way or the second way or the third way. It is the only way for us. It is the British way."

Political heavyweights awake in time for the big sleep

SAMUEL TAYLOR COLERIDGE once said, "Men should be weighed, not counted."

He was, of course, questioning whether democracy was a privilege on which less politically aware folk should be entitled to express an opinion or have a vote! But I wondered what he would have made of the commencement, this week, of the annual "Parliamentary weigh-in".

I decided to join in. I saw it as my chance to tough it out with the political heavyweights in a small Committee room down in the bowels of the Palace of Westminster.

The event was being sponsored to raise money for Save the Children—justification in itself, I thought. The "weigh-in" will take place once a week until Christmas and is also intended to give Weight Watchers a chance to encourage MPs to adopt a healthier lifestyle.

The air was thick as I arrived; probably because the Billy Bunter fan club members present had been instructed to remove their shoes before stepping up to the scales.

Where weight is concerned, self-image is everything. As I stepped up I imagined deep humiliation as a summer of heavy Cornish fare had probably taken its toll. Would I be able to ease my portly frame up to the scales without causing a by-election, I worried.

But my arrival prompted an entirely different reaction:

"Fraud!" shouted one Sumo look-a-like. "Disgrace!" chimed another. "Bet he has to run around in the shower to get wet," protested another wag.

"But, it's for a good cause," I retorted, cheesily.

Harmony returned when we all agreed that I'd probably expire before I won the Christmas weight loss competition, and I was allowed to pass.

BY THE TIME you read this article I imagine that the Jenkins Commission will have finally pronounced on electoral reform.[1]

Now, before your eyes glaze over or you hurriedly turn to the sports pages I have an exclusive admission.

Though I am a Liberal Democrat MP, I do not believe that statements on electoral and constitutional reform are anticipated more eagerly than the World Cup draw or the votes for the Eurovision Song contest.

I have often watched in utter horror as Constitutional enthusiasts clear whole buildings by rising to their feet, or transform poor unwitting victims from energetic vitality into deep coma at the mere utterance of the words "single transferable vote".

There's something strangely hypnotic about the subject. Most normal people attempt to count their shirt buttons when the subject is announced. But buttons become sheep and, before you know it, you're putty in the hands of the "Land of Nod".

I often advise anyone wanting a quiet night out in a popular, busy pub to announce on arrival, "I want to talk to you all about constitutional issues…" and then watch the place clear. The Landlord, if alert enough, will quite rightly ban you for life, but you'll be amazed at how effective it is.

Constitutionalists in the Commons are assumed to have contracted a particularly unpleasant form of leprosy. One of my dear colleagues who "bores for Britain" on the subject—though not naturally reclusive —can normally be seen wandering around the Palace of Westminster with furlongs of personal space around him.

In this context, turning "the Jenkins Commission" into a conversation piece rather than a conversation stopper is clearly a challenge for all politicians who seriously believe that we can improve our accountability by embracing sensible change.

"NEVER apologise. Never explain", advised one very experienced MP when I approached him to apologise and explain why I had misinterpreted his intervention on a speech I made in the Commons during the early days.

Whilst this kind of tough, "brazen-it-out-at-all-costs" attitude is clearly the one to adopt if you want to be accepted as a stereotypical MP, I have decided to seize the opportunity of my mistakes—many as they are—to demonstrate my fallibility and humanity (it could take up all my time!).

And so it is, that, with a quiet sprinkling of pride, but a large helping of humble pie, I apologise following my last proffering to this column.

Because pointing up the failings of my own breed in the Commons backfired unintentionally on the good people of the Isles of Scilly.

The apology letters caused by my rantings have, I hope, gone at least a small way to assuring both sides of a regrettable matter on Scilly that I intended only to wound my own kind and not any Scillonian resident.

27th October 1998

[1] *The "Jenkins Report" (Independent Commission on the Voting System) was published in October 1998. The Commission's central recommendation was that the best alternative for Britain to the first-past-the-post (FPTP) system is a two-vote mixed system which can be described as either limited AMS [Additional Member System] or Alternative Vote plus additional members.*

Taking Matthew Parris on an outing
to the real world

I **SEE** you've been 'outed' by Matthew Parris," said a colleague as I breezed into the Whip's Office. Panicking, I rapidly checked the columns of *The Times* and there it was.[1]

(Matthew Parris, the highly regarded, terrifyingly articulate—and self-'outed'—former Tory MP is also renowned for the almost obscene pleasure he takes in trying to cut and wound others.)

Yes, on page 2, I found that I had been 'outed' for asking a serious question at Prime Minister's Question Time, rather than the tawdry little one he would have preferred me to ask.

I had asked the Prime Minister for his support for a British withdrawal from the Multilateral Agreement on Investment (M.A.I). Journalists, who believe that the private life of another is always a priority for attention, rarely recognise the significance of a complex, remote, poorly understood but potentially devastating international policy agreement; especially one which would give multinational companies unfettered rights without any enforceable responsibilities.

For the apparently rarefied group of enthusiasts who follow these things, this question should have been both timely and significant, even if it failed to illicit a meaningful answer from Tony Blair.[2]

But the massed ranks of journalists in the Press Gallery weren't "watching the lips" of the men and women talking policy; they were rummaging through the garbage bins of their private lives.

I have often assumed that the rubbish this kind of journalism generates is what the general public wants. But I now realise that it's what the press want. Because trying to understand complex international agreements is hard work.

Even in enlightened, liberal West Cornwall and Scilly, although I get bags of mail expressing concern about the M.A.I., I do, very occasionally, get the less appetising "disgusted of Tunbridge Wells" style letter which merely betrays an unhealthy obsession with the things other consenting adults choose to do to in their private lives.

This fascination in the private lives of others completely passes me by. In any case, what kind of headlines are the press trying to generate?

"SHOCK NEWS : We are not all the same!"; "BELIEVE IT OR

NOT: Some people are different from others!"

Surely I can't be alone in thinking—whatever the inclination of the people concerned—it is all pretty stomach churning stuff. News of this kind of thing can put you right off your breakfast cereal.

THE CROWDS surrounding the Palace of Westminster during the last week—making it the biggest continual vigil I have seen around the building since being elected—are not there to pry into the private lives of public figures, but to seek justice for the public actions of a former dictator who would rather keep it all private.

There had been a lot of punching the air with both hands around the House of Commons at the news that former Chilean dictator, General Augusto Pinochet, had given himself up to the police rather than face the prospect of having to take more afternoon tea with Baroness Thatcher.

The Law Lords have been taking evidence in the appeal against a Court ruling that General Pinochet's arrest had been unlawful. Pinochet faces charges in Spain of genocide, torture and terrorism after the military coup which overthrew the Allende Government in 1973.

What I wonder, si if we send him hom just how Chile w his reception be

On learning of his arrest we heard that General Pinochet was hurt and bewildered. The word "tough" and the word "cheese" are among the more moderate to spring to mind when hearing of his pleadings.

No doubt, by the time this column is published, he will have secured his appeal and scarpered back off to Chile.[3]

10th November 1998

[1] *Matthew Parris "outed" the then Trade & Industry Secretary Peter Mandelson as gay on Newsnight a week earlier. The reference to Andrew George's question was contained in The Times on 5th November 1998.*
[2] [3] *See Appendix, page 181.*

Lords a-leaping into the "long grass"

THE WORLD had turned completely upside down.

Unelected Hereditary Peers had cast themselves as the only true defenders of real democracy; the Conservatives as the proponents of a purer form of electoral reform which, if you believe it, the Liberal Democrats (no less) were determined to resist.[1]

The European Parliamentary Elections Bill had previously seemed a relatively innocuous thing which appeared to have the words "inevitability" written all over it.

But whilst MPs and Lords were working themselves into a lather of mutual antagonism, the Commons cleaning staff—who I consult on these matters, as the people who most closely reflect public opinion— could hardly contain their indifference.

The progress of the Bill was an exhibition of how sport can degenerate into gamesmanship. It first started as a respectable game of chess, which then became a frenetic ping-pong between the Lords and Commons until it concluded as an ignominious contest of "chicken".

When we all came out from the intensity of the Palace of Westminster blinking into the cool night air of reality, we shouldn't have been surprised to find a public (those who weren't sensibly tucked up in bed) at best bemused and at worst angry at the antics of grown men and women in the nation's Houses of Parliament.

And the result?

Well, the Lords had made the best case for their own abolition, which the Government has now brought forward, and the Commons had demonstrated a need for a proper independent second chamber to scrutinize its work.

DURING my childhood, in the south of this Constituency—in the days when everyone was "Pard"[2] and before Cornish self mocking humour was mistaken for imbecility—I remember being one of the large George "invasion" of the local chapel on a Sunday morning.

We were, of course, sermonised on the virtues of tolerance, understanding, selflessness and of charity. "Charity begins at home" was a regular theme for Methodists then, just as it is today. They were four very carefully chosen words and had a very clear meaning.

I remember that it was during the long dark winter of the 1980s that I found that phrases learnt in childhood could dramatically change their meaning. Charity still began at home, but it ended there too. Charity began with "Number One" and only occasionally stretched to "number two" ("the Missis", a close friend, the dog, etc.,) on a good day.

"Charity begins at home" became the oft repeated rallying cry of the "Charity ends at home" Brigade. The Brigade's secret motto was: "Scorn begins outside the garden gate" which was customarily heaped upon the intended victims (the homeless, unemployed, asylum seekers, etc.) of the policies of the day, with little pause for reflection.

As for the poor of the Third World, well, they were "dead meat" to this Brigade and, with the assistance of some very dubious arms sales policies and exploitative trading practices, they too often were.

THE GOVERNMENT'S Queen's Speech—being debated this week—provided an opportunity radically to reform the country, away from the programme of the "Charity ends at home" Brigade.

We are now entering the all important second Parliamentary session of the new Government. To me the legislative programme appears to have become all too timid. The reform of the Lords will take up most of the year and will probably be a pretty unedifying spectacle.

The Government's priorities are now being judged by whether radical reform has been, in Commons' parlance, kicked "into the long grass". Missed opportunities of electoral reform, social security reform, parliamentary scrutiny of arms export licences, a Royal Commission into animal welfare and action to meet greenhouse gas reduction targets are amongst many priorities which have been put on hold. The Lords would like to leap out there too. But, as Commons' wags have put it, "there is standing room only in the long grass"—until, we presume, the House of Lords has been reformed.

1st December 1998

[1] *Some had accused the Liberal Democrats of supporting the Government's Euro Election Bill, which included a "closed list" system in exchange for being "given a job" on the Joint Cabinet Committee. Liberal Democrats rejected this, arguing that although the proposed system was not their preferred form of proportional representation they would not vote against the Bill because if it were lost then they risked being left with the old first past the post system.*
[2] *Cornish dialect for partner or friend.*

Lording it with the sick parrots

MY SPECULATION of "Lords a-leaping" *(The Cornishman 3rd December 1998)* appears to have been more prophetic than even I had anticipated.

After centuries of draping themselves around the red benches in a variety of semi-comatose contortions, during the last week it has been as much as we Commoners can do to dissuade their Lordships from collective acts of chivalrous hara-kiri. Attempting to stop Lords leaping on their own swords has become a major preoccupation for MPs who have experienced collective sympathy for the beleaguered peers after poor Lord Cranborne was savagely set upon by a deranged Mr Hague.[1]

Until recently I am sure that most people had simply assumed that the House of Lords existed primarily as a museum for foreign tourists. Some, so I understand, were adamant that it provides a picturesque backdrop for public health information films providing salutary warnings about imprudent positions of repose. "If you sleep like that, you could end up looking like this!" was the subliminal message derived by some.

But, in fact, a surprising number of their Lordships are wide-awake for a fair proportion of the day. Never more so than over the last week.

THE EXCITEMENT generated by the earlier Euro Elections Bill[2] had been quickly surpassed by negotiations around the proposed reform of the Lords.

Pillows were left with shooting sticks in the corridors and lobbies. Peers were sitting bolt upright. Speculation mounted about whether the luxurious, softly upholstered red benches would survive the uncharacteristic pummelling of a pulsating House. The activity in the Lords Chamber was making the Commons look positively restrained and sober.

Other than the hereditaries, the House of Lords has been described by various MPs as the place where "political has-beens are put out to grass" or "the ideal rest home for the semi-clapped out".

However, recent events demonstrate a deep cultural distinction between the two Houses. Because when, like Mr Hague, you've immersed yourself in the political culture of the Commons and generated a thirst for point scoring at any cost, you become unable to recognise a cross bench political solution, even when it sits up and "scats"[3] you between the eyes.

To be fair the Lords has an established culture of reflection, compromise, dealing and working for the best practical effect. The House of Lords always looks uncomfortable when it is dragooned into doing the dirty work of the opposition party in the Commons and only makes itself look weak and foolish. It is that recognition which has created the backlash from the more thoughtful of the opposition bench peers.

I believe a solution to the need for sensible reform of the Lords is possible but not under terms set only by the political culture of the Commons.

I HAVE recently come back from a brief "diplomatic" mission to one of the former eastern block countries seeking to be in the first wave of eastern European entrants to the E.U.

Yes, the British Parliamentary football team took on the might of the much more youthful parliamentarians of Hungary.

I could fill all the pages of *The Cornishman* with excuses as to why we stood little chance of winning but suffice it to say that it would have been undiplomatic to have accepted the hospitality of the Hungarians and then to have beaten them on their own soil, in the Ferencváros Stadium live on Hungarian television!

Throughout much of the game their team was 100 years younger than ours and included former professional footballers and athletes.

To demonstrate how unfit our team was, I was considered to be one of the fittest and one of only a few to have played the full 90 minutes! I think you're getting the picture by now.

A carefully choreographed lunge at their young Speaker, which took man, ball and half of the turf on our half of the field, ensured that I gave away a judicious penalty from which their former international opened the scoring.

Fortunately, a goal rout didn't follow and we finished the losers by 2 goals to nil.

While we were "sick as parrots" the Hungarians were "over the moon". Or so it seemed when the 35 year old Hungarian Prime Minister Viktor Orban—a very useful footballer himself—thanked us after the game.

In footballing parlance, just as the Lords will find, it was a game of two haves; the "haves" and the "have nots".

8th December 1998

[1]   The Conservative Party was split in December 1998 when William Hague was forced to sack Lord Cranborne, his Leader in the House of Lords, after an unauthorised "backstairs" deal with Labour over the abolition of hereditary voting rights. Hague wanted to reject any deal until stage two of a reformed Lords was agreed.
[2]   The Lords rejected the European Election Bill six times in the 1997/98 and 1998/99 Parliamentary sessions. The Bill proposed a "closed list" system of proportional representation that was opposed by the Lords. It was eventually forced through under the Parliament Act in December 1998.
[3]   "Scat" is a Cornish language / dialect word for "hit".

Early football beginnings with Mullion CP School Football Team: Peter Tonkin, Hamish Wilson, Robin Gilmour, Tim George (brother), Sidney Rosevear, Paul Lawer, Martin Wilson, Bruce Bennets, Keith Pilgrim, Andrew George (age 9), David Hatton and Carl Bray.

Resigned to a season of peace keeping

THE CHAMBER was in deeply solemn rather than festive mood as it rose for the Christmas recess.

The House was debating a Government motion on the pre-emptive bombings of military installations in Iraq.

The language and syntax used was, as usual, remote, impersonal, third person, clinical. The bombs were "surgical strikes", the prospects of any other damage or killing was "collateral" and we of course had no argument with the Iraqi people.

As there was no opportunity to vote on the issue the debate itself became pretty academic.

We had debated it before. Early this year I was one of two Liberal Democrat MPs who could not support the strategy of the threat of military action at that stage.[1]

Whilst I am not a pacifist and strongly believe that our "defence" forces now have a role providing a major contribution to the goal of seeking "world peace", we need to be clear when military action is appropriate.

I am a strong supporter of the men and women who are prepared to put their lives at risk in defence of peace and democracy and against those who perpetrate the most hideous crimes. I will always give our troops my fullest backing. Now as at any other time.

But, at the same time, we must be clear about when and why we engage our forces. They should not be engaged ineptly or inappropriately.

I agree that Saddam Hussein appears to be one of the most evil people on earth. Our quarrel is with him and not the Iraqi people. He must be stopped. Whilst appropriate military action must be among the options for action it should be within the context of an international strategy to control the prospects of any build up of weapons of mass destruction in Iraq.

I am not sure that the decision taken before Christmas had achieved the international backing we should have sought. My quarrel is over the competence of the decision-making process rather than the decision itself.

IF WE ARE conveying peace and goodwill to all, then I doubt that Peter Mandelson nor Geoffrey Robinson would have received much peace or goodwill this Christmas.[2]

I prefer to see resignations based on political judgement rather than judgements made on the private lives of politicians. Though the demonisation of both of these former Ministers no doubt added to the hunger for "sleaze" against them, I am sure that their decision to resign was appropriate and honourable.

24th December 1998

[1]   Andrew George and his Parliamentary colleague—Norman Baker—defied strong direction to vote with the Government on the 17th February 1998 over the bombing of Iraq.
[2]   Trade Secretary Peter Mandelson MP resigned on the 23rd December 1998 after it emerged he had taken, but not declared, a £373,000 loan from Paymaster General Geoffrey Robinson MP, who also resigned.

From Andrew George's Christmas card, a design by his son Davy.

Trying to spin in the dewy syrup of ecstasy

MARTIN BELL—the white suited Independent MP for Tatton—sent shock waves across the back benches this week, when he revealed that he regretted his pledge not to stay as an MP for more than one term, because he was, allegedly, "enjoying" himself.[1]

Like me, many MPs have spent months—others have spent years—carefully nurturing the clear image in the minds of their constituents that life in the Palace of Westminster is one of "sackcloth and ashes"; intolerable demands which inevitably lead to weeks on end of sleep-deprived, inescapable, high pressure torture. Sorrow and sympathy are the reactions sought—not envy.

MPs who attempt to speak the truth generate the same homicidal yearnings from their colleagues as do those who seem to always keep a pristine, tidy and paper free desk. In the voting lobby on the following day I seized my opportunity to sort the matter out when Martin Bell joined the Liberal Democrats for a vote on the Government's handling of the funding crisis in the NHS.

I puffed myself up into a Neil-and-Christine-Hamilton-ill-met-on-Tatton-Common-impression, but with a real get-even attitude.

Cornering him against the oak and leather bound book panelled walls of the opulent lobby, I confronted him with the truth.

"But I squared it with my Chief Whip," protested the Commons' sole independent MP.

Reeling from this near fatal knock-out punch so early in round one I managed to come back with:

"But what about the implications? Hadn't you consulted a spin doctor first?"

The acclaimed former war and foreign correspondent had no answer. He attempted to mouth objections but knew that modern-day political reality was a devastating counter-punch.

Seriously, of course, Martin Bell is absolutely right. Though there are many and diverse pressures, the fact is that the lot of the MP is one of immense privilege and opportunity. Could anyone with an ardent thirst for the chance to explore, engage in and even influence the debate of the day and the affairs of the country (and be paid to do it!) not, in all honesty, admit that it must be one of the most enjoyable jobs.

Those who try to pretend otherwise either suffer the affliction of over-blown self-importance (Latin name: *pompositus egotistica*) or their unquenchable personal ambition and thirst for power will always leave them miserable.

AS MOST of us know, the job of the "spin doctor" is to control the story of politics. A good spin doctor has a ready supply of good and bad stories to spoon feed the babbling, credulous nursery of young lobby journalists. Privileged "briefings", "leaks" and "exclusive" news offers are the irresistible trade marks of the spin-doctor.

A much admired Parliamentary colleague, Paul Flynn (MP for Newport West), says in his book *"Commons Knowledge"*[2] that the attention span of a spin doctor is that of a retarded earthworm. "Nirvana to them is a happy headline in tabloids tomorrow. The day after tomorrow and the rest of the future is an invisible, far over their time horizon."

So it has been with Government announcements about the Health Service in recent months. If every promise of new spending commitments were indeed new money then the country would have been bankrupted in mega-Brazilian style[3] long ago.

Soon enough the truth will catch up with the spin, but it's difficult when Parliament is so often by-passed by Government.

ONE OF MY earliest lessons about this place was to recognise the desperate need to give Parliament a proper and more rigorous role in scrutinising the activities and pronouncements of Government.

If the job of the independent and critical minds of the Commons chamber is to "tell the truth that dare not speak its name", then it becomes almost impossible to do so when a spin doctor has slipped a different version of it on to the front pages of the morning's tabloids without coming to Parliament first.

19th January 1999

[1]   Martin Bell won Tatton as an Independent MP on an anti-corruption ticket. This was the week that he confirmed "reluctantly" that he would stand by his election pledge not to contest the seat again. However, he was eventually persuaded to stand, unsuccessfully, as an Independent candidate for Brentwood and Ongar at the 2001 General Election. Also see Martin Bell "An Accidental MP" (2000).
[2]   Paul Flynn, Commons Knowledge: How to be a Backbencher, 1997 (p. 140)
[3]   The International Monetary Fund promised $41 billion to Brazil in November 1998 to help it stabilise its currency, the real. By mid January 1999 the real plummeted by nearly 10% and on the 15th January 1999 was devalued again after Brazil had used around $40 billion of foreign exchange reserves to defend the currency. The Brazil debacle follows IMF programme failures in Thailand (August 1997), Indonesia (November 1997), Korea (December 1997) and Russia (August 1998).

Fishing for popularity with the Flat Earth Society

THIS WEEK I welcome fellow members of the Agriculture Select Committee to our constituency. They are here with me as part of our Inquiry into the fishing industry.[1]

I will start by telling them about Wally. Now, Wally was a great "character" from the fishing village of my birth and up-bringing—Mullion in the South of the constituency. Like him my family had a small open boat for mackerel hand-lining and potting. He was always gaming around and he knew that we knew that when he spun a tale for a group of visitors, he would never let a few home truths get in the way of a jolly good story.

Amongst the most hilarious was the one he used to tell about the time he was caught out at sea alone in an unexpected storm...

...He saw the raging waves easily breaking over the harbour walls. What hope was there of getting home in this weather? If he tried to enter the harbour mouth the boat would surely be smashed to pieces. So with his courage in one hand and controlling the boat with the other, he got on a wave which took him over the harbour wall and placed him (boat and all) delicately on the slipway. By now his philosophical delivery, his pause (whilst he slowly puffed at his pipe), his modest reassurance that it wasn't all down to his courage and skill had helped to create the classic theatrical moment. His anxious listeners would by now have suspended all disbelief.

That is, apart from the locals who knew better. But most visitors would prefer to listen to Wally lest their dreams be dashed, as his little boat would have been, on the harbour wall.

IT'S A LITTLE like this with the state of the present debate on the fishing industry.

A matter of weeks ago the annual pre-Christmas Commons fishing debate provided us with the best opportunity for the year to set out our political stall and put party policy to the test.

Curiously, only I, as Liberal Democrat fisheries spokesman, had placed an alternative to Government policy on the Order Paper[2]. After 18 years in Government the official opposition had nothing to say.

This was surprising as the previous Government had added to the burdens on the industry, failed to invest in the UK fleet, brought forward Spanish access to western waters by six years and failed to take decisive action to reduce the loss of fishing quotas to "flag of convenience" vessels, amongst other felonies.

I simply set out the consistent approach we've taken for years:

- to scrap the over centralised basis of E.U. policy by handing more power back to fishermen and fishing stakeholders in Europe's fishing regions;
- to safeguard the 6- and 12-mile limits and our coastal waters;
- to take sustainable fishing methods—like Cornish Mackerel Handling—out of the quota system altogether;
- to strengthen partnerships between fishermen, scientists and environmental groups,
- to ensure equality of monitoring and enforcement across Europe through bi-lateral arrangements; and
- to oppose the imposition of the E.U. Working Time Directive on the industry, as proposed by the Labour Government.

IN CONTRAST, after 18 years of supporting his Party's policy when in Government, within nano-seconds of taking the portfolio the Conservative's spokesman concluded that they could simply have pulled out of the CFP after all. Simple as that!

Well, one thing was simple, and it wasn't pulling out of the CFP.

Desirable as it arguably may be, it's simply not possible. Every attempt to illicit an answer as to how it could be done was met with either a blank look or a change of subject. Since that time we have received an insight to an answer.

I think we're being asked seriously to believe that going to Europe and doing a rather silly looking British-Bulldog-wielding-a-handbag impression will see all other E.U. nations pleading submission.

Now we saw how successful that approach was with the allegedly "resolute" stance of non-cooperation over the British Beef Export ban during the last Government; it resulted in a waste of valuable time and a humiliating climb down.

The pitiful truth is that putting the Tories in charge of British Fishing Policy in Europe would be like making Glen Hoddle Minister for the Disabled.[3]

However, what would have surprised an objective observer of last

December's debate was that this view has been given the credence of some of the media and acres of column inches in one regional paper.

The analysis of the ills of the industry and criticisms of the failures of the CFP were well made. I couldn't agree more. But, as Churchill might have said, "The CFP is the worst fishing policy, apart from all the others."[4] Because, apart from the, as ever, entirely sensible and responsible views attributed to the Cornish Fishermen's P.O., the rest of the news about the debate read as if a reporter had stumbled in on a meeting of the Flat Earth Society.

If only life were that simple. Calling for the repatriation of fishing policy on these terms is a little like asking the Indian Government if it would now kindly come back under British Colonial rule or asking women if they wouldn't mind giving up their right to vote.

Even Wally, with all his arts and ways, could not have made this nonsense sound convincing.

Western Morning News, 2nd February 1999

[1]   *Sea Fishing, 8th Report of the Agricultural Select Committee, 5th August 1999.*
[2]   *Fisheries, House of Commons Hansard Debates, 15th December 1998*
[3]   *Glen Hoddle was sacked as England coach on Tuesday 2nd February 1999. Hoddle admitted that he had made a "serious error of judgement" in his remarks about reincarnation and disability. His comments were reported in The Times of 30th January 1999 where he said, "You and I have physically been given two hands and two legs and half-decent brains. Some people have not been born like that for a reason. The karma is working from another lifetime. I have nothing to hide about that. It's not only people with disabilities. What you sow, you have to reap.".*
[4]   *"No one pretends that democracy is perfect or all-wise. Indeed, it has been said that democracy is the worst form of government except all those other forms that have been tried from time to time." Winston [Leonard Spencer] Churchill, 1874–1965.*

Wrestling with genetically modified arguments

REPORTS OF obscenity from the U.S. Senate may have taken our eye off the ball.[1]

An obscene amount of public money and time had been spent on poking noses into private lives.

Meanwhile, back on earth, as Westminster politicians know it, genetic modification in Government Ministers' arguments seemed to stifle the independent thought of some.

Claims that some Ministers overindulged on politically modified links with companies that had an interest in genetic modification were strongly denied.

Questions I had raised in the Select Committee[2] over the last year suddenly became interesting. When I had questioned Ministers on this before, it was treated like a barely tolerable interlude in otherwise serious proceedings. While other members counted shirt buttons, Ministers had dismissed concerns as misinformed and out of touch.

The fact is that being invited to push back the frontiers of science can itself be very seductive. We had been just as confident about Thalidomide once—but at least we could take that off the shelf when the full tragedy and horror of the mistake became clear.

Not so with genetically modified crops. Once out in the environment they could cross-fertilise to their little hearts' desire.

Far better that millions of dollars of public money is spent probing the lives of genetically modified seeds, foods and food products, rather than the private lives of the people who should be concentrating on these questions.

Politicians should wrestle with the real questions which affect people's lives and that's why I'm going back to the Select Committee this week to demand an Inquiry into Genetically Modified Organisms (GMOs).

16th February 1999

[1] *Total news and comment column inches from 22nd to 28th January in*
The Guardian, The Times, The Daily Telegraph, The Independant, The Sunday Times,

The Observer and The Daily Mail included 225 inches on King Hussein's illness, 242 on Jack Straw's comments on adoption, 351.5 on the Irish Peace Process, 419 on Paddy Ashdown's retirement and 849 on allegations regarding President Clinton's private affair. Statistics taken from The Guardian, 30th January 1999.

[2]   As well as Select Committee reports, MAFF's Annual report, see also "Genetically Modified Organisms", 6th Report of the Agricultural Select Committee, 15th June 1999.

When doing nothing is not an option

IT WAS AS SOMBRE an occasion as I can ever remember. The Commons Chamber usually haemorrhages a sea of grey suits immediately after Prime Minister's Questions (PMQs) on a Wednesday afternoon at 3.30, leaving vast prairies of green benches no matter what the debate or Ministerial statement afterwards.

But today it was different.

I believe that more entered than left the chamber on this afternoon to hear the Home Secretary. In a clamorous silence which contrasted with the hooliganism of PMQs moments before, Jack Straw, in the deadest of deadpan voices, announced the findings of the Inquiry into the racist murder of Stephen Lawrence in Eltham, London, six years ago.[1]

Mouths dropped. Heads shook in despair. We sat in shame and horror. Edmund Burke said that "All it takes for evil to triumph is for good men to do nothing". That guilt lay heavily on us all.

An innocent young black man brutally murdered by racists. His family very badly let down. And now a nation shamed.

BUT THIS was the same chamber which had given the Immigration and Asylum Bill a fair wind only days before. The language used against asylum seekers has always, in my view, gone beyond rational examination of their claims and has entered the realms of scapegoating.

Britain doesn't have a "flood" of bogus asylum seekers planning to "sponge" off the "gravy train" of state "hand outs". In some years we have as many people trying to leave this country as trying to get in.

We have, relative to many other western countries, small numbers of asylum seekers and most of them are from well-known trouble spots like Bosnia and Somalia. But most of what we hear about asylum seekers is the hysteria based either on ignorance or a wilful desire to distort the truth.

WITHOUT doubt, the most upsetting and insulting thing anyone has said to me about the Cornwall we all love is, "I have come down here to get away from the blacks."

Apart from demonstrating a seriously diseased mind, (as a Cornishman I am proud of our tradition of Liberal moderation and religious and political non-conformity), I find this kind of remark particularly offensive. It jolts me out of complacency.

The question is: what kind of image are we creating to give the impression that Cornwall is a safe haven for racists? It's probably because we fail to contradict these when they utter their detestable views ("for evil to triumph…").

People don't unburden their racist prejudices upon me these days; not since I took on the Liberal Democrat tag publicly, with its proud tradition of anti-racism and anti-apartheid. But when they used to come out with those loathsome words, I have to admit to taking some pleasure in minutely describing the barren, deserted island I felt they should take themselves off to.

When you look into the narrow eyes and the tiny mind of a racist you invariable see a sadness and deep hatred.

Me am beth hanow heb dewath ha bry bisqwethack rag nerra …

LAST WEEK I successfully called for a Commons debate on the Cornish language. It was in relation to the European Charter on Minority Languages.[2] I was pleased that it received a positive response from Members and the Foreign Office Minister who responded.

What we know, and they acknowledged, was that the Cornish

language is not a symbol of narrow isolationism (though a handful of people would prefer it that way) but of our own contribution to the celebration of diversity of cultures, identities and languages throughout the British Isles and Europe.

[Andrew George MP was a founder and is now President of the Council for Racial Equality in Cornwall—He is also a Trustee of the national Rural Race Equality Project.]

2nd March 1999

[1]   In April 1993 Stephen Lawrence, aged 18, was stabbed to death by a gang at a bus stop in Eltham, South-East London. The murder was recorded as "racially motivated" but charges against the white suspects were dropped due to "insufficient evidence". In April 1994 new evidence uncovered by Stephen Lawrence's family was ruled "insufficient to support murder charges" by the Crown Prosecution Service. In April 1996 the private prosecution brought by the Lawrence family against three young men collapsed after Mr Justice Curtis ruled that vital eyewitness evidence was inadmissible. In February 1997 the Inquest into the death of Stephen Lawrence began. The jury soon returned a verdict of unlawful killing. The front page of the Daily Mail carried the banner headline, "Murderers" and the names and photographs of five men who, it said, killed Stephen Lawrence in 1993. The Mail challenged them to sue it for libel. In June 1997 the then Home Secretary—Jack Straw—met the parents of Stephen Lawrence. His Conservative predecessor, Michael Howard, had refused to do so.
In August 1997 Jack Straw announced a full Independent Judicial Inquiry into the handling by the police and Crown Prosecution Service of the murder of Stephen Lawrence headed by the former High Court Judge, Sir William Macpherson.
The report accused the Metropolitan Police of "pernicious and institutionalised racism". It criticised the Metropolitan Police Commissioner, Sir Paul Condon, and made 70 recommendations, encompassing law and race-awareness education, including changing the law so that suspects can be re-tried if new evidence emerges.
[2]   'Cornish Language', House of Commons Hansard Debates, 23rd February 1999

Our Objective One is a "new beginning"

BARRING a mass resignation of EU leaders in Berlin, or the engagement of gun boats to resolve the banana trade war with the US, Cornwall and Scilly should have finally confirmed our status as a European region worthy of the highest level of European aid by the end of this week. Objective One status will have been secured.[1]

Amid the popping corks of Cornish mead, cider, wine, real ale and spring water will be much deserved pats on the back for all concerned in the campaign.

To be fair it should be recorded as a triumph for the Government as well as local authorities and MPs. It is also an unquestionable triumph for Cornwall's Euro MP, Robin Teverson, who has fought so long and hard for this. But, above all, it is a triumph for the people of Cornwall and Scilly whose poverty has gone unrecognised for far too long.

After all of this celebration and mutual congratulation we will have to get down to the serious task in hand. In doing this we need to recognise that the inappropriate use of over £600 million of public funds could do Cornwall and Scilly a lot of damage as well as some significant good.

I HAVE TO ADMIT that one of the biggest problems I have in discussing economic development "strategies", "visions", "missions", etc., is just how bland and insubstantial most of the language used is. Much emphasis has been put upon Cornwall's need for a "can do" culture for business.

Well, I don't think anyone is going to disagree with that. For example, I haven't heard anyone arguing for a "can't do" culture for business.

Part of the problem of past economic development strategies—which clearly must have failed, otherwise we wouldn't be in this mess—is that they were based upon an unstated belief that Cornwall is fundamentally flawed because it is not sufficiently like other places.

The old analysis suggested that Cornwall is:
- Small—too small to be taken seriously;
- Remote—and geographically weak;

● Backward and undynamic.

I think now, and with the benefit of hindsight, we may conclude that in fact Cornwall was OK, may have been OK all along, but that it was the policy direction from Whitehall which was fundamentally flawed. It may just have been that the strategies were the product of small, remote, backward and undynamic minds.[2]

INSTEAD of seeing Cornwall and Scilly as a series of weaknesses (small, remote, backward, etc) a new Objective One programme should start afresh and look at the strengths—strong identity, environment, history, culture, maritime links, positive consumer image, resourcefulness of its people, etc).

We should challenge the cosy assumptions of the past and build a plan which will motivate and inspire.

We could end up in seven years time with a whole lot of new tarmac linking us to a South West Region which decides the future for Cornwall, but with little else to show for the money we've had.

Or we could set ourselves challenges which build on our strengths and distinctiveness.

For my part I believe we would have failed if we had not:

1) established a University College;

2) produced a nationally recognised and successful "Cornish brand" image; and

3) made Cornwall Britain's "green peninsula" for environmentally sustainable technologies and products.

Clear and determined. Building on our strengths, rather than seeking to overcome our perceived weaknesses. Cornwall and the Isles of Scilly could use this opportunity as a new beginning. A chance to rebuild the self-confidence we once lost.

23rd March 1999

[1] On 25th March 1999, Cornwall and Scilly were designated as an Objective One region.

[2] Andrew George previously wrote along these lines with Bernard Deacon and Ronald Perry in "Cornwall at the Crossroads" 1988. ISBN 0 9513918 0 1.

The "benefit of hindsight" on the Kosovo/British border

IT IS often said that "the benefit of hindsight is a wonderful thing". The politically bankrupt believe it is a marvellous gift with which they are especially endowed. The rest of us see it as a false moral high ground occupied by bar room bores, armchair footballers and the like.

The appalling crisis in the Balkans has given those MPs with this amazing sixth sense an opportunity for us to experience the full benefit of their exceptional talents.

We are told the Government "should have done this" and "shouldn't have done that". Of course, none of this advice was available when decisions were being taken.

It is—I believe properly—accepted practice that when the country is engaged in war, opposition parties offer the Government constructive support—unless they are clearly opposed to the action. This support was resoundingly given when the Government decided to join the NATO action against Milosevic.

But this has broken down since and, jumping up from political depths rarely seen even in this chamber, the "benefit of hindsight merchants" have risen to the occasion by lowering the tone of debate.

Now, four weeks ago there were (mainly Labour) back benchers who questioned the military action (Benn, Corbyn, Mahon, Dalyell and others), but this was on the basis of NATO's authority to act. No one warned or predicted the potential of the escalation of Milosevic's action against the Kosovars.[1]

True, contingencies should have been prepared for this possible outcome, but that should not be a matter of political point scoring.

If we failed, then we all failed—those who brazenly enjoy the luxury of hindsight as well as the Government itself.

BUT THERE is one other hypocrisy we could dwell on and it is a matter in which the Conservative hindsight experts are just as culpable as the present Labour Government. It is the hypocrisy of scapegoating so called "bogus" asylum seekers.

The bottom line is that the past Tory Government and the present New Labour Government with its new Immigration and Asylum

Bill[2] have played into the hands of the worst kind of narrow-minded tabloid campaign.

I THINK we all agree that we would not want to admit asylum seekers who are allegedly "bogus"—i.e. people who, we are told, seek to "cheat" their way here, to "sponge" off us and "take advantage" of our welcome to live "comfortably off" on our over-generous benefit system.

But the present law and this Government's Bill would penalise genuine as well as bogus asylum seekers. Britain has imposed visa restrictions on states like Bosnia and Colombia from which large numbers of genuine—not "bogus"— asylum seekers flee.

A Kosovar refugee must get a visa in person from the British Embassy in Belgrade—which is closed due to war! Even if it were open he would have to cross Serbia but would not be given a visa if he told the truth. Britain refuses visas to those who say they want to come to Heathrow to claim asylum.

If he attempts to cheat his way in he would be thrown off a plane or a lorry, etc., because carriers who transport asylum seekers without correct papers are fined.

In short there is no legal way for an honest Kosovar refugee to reach the shores of this great and proud country of freedom and democracy.

Kosovars don't have visas because Milosevic has made sure that they have been stripped of their passports, marriage documents and birth certificates. They have no way of proving who they say they are, which suits the ethnic cleansers in Belgrade and the Government and right wing press in London.

A LACK of papers and a reliance on illegal entry ensures that the unscrupulous can characterise the "genuine" as "bogus".

Perhaps (I hope against experience), perhaps instead of using the "talent" of the benefit of hindsight to score tawdry political points, perhaps we should use that benefit of hindsight to review our treatment of asylum seekers and find an honest and humane solution to the need for fair asylum and immigration rules.

If we had the moral strength and the benefit of foresight we could do something about this.

19th April 1999

[1] "Kosovo", *House of Commons Hansard Debates, 23rd March 1999.*
[2]   *The Immigration and Asylum Act eventually received Royal Assent on 11th November 1999.*

On the gravy train to nowhere

SHORTLY AFTER I was elected to Parliament, two years ago now, an old friend came up to me with the congratulation: "how long will it take before that nice Mr George becomes an unprincipled sleaze ball like the rest of them up there?" (Meaning, I supposed, all MPs in Westminster.)

I suggested that I would resist the temptations for at least a couple of nano-seconds before eventually succumbing to the irresistible pressure.

Of course, the reality of having a 12,000 letter per annum in-tray, a multitude of major campaigns, a significant spokesmanship and having to compete with a select band of superhuman beings with silver tongues and encyclopaedias for brains is a pretty fair diversion.

Indeed, it was while on duty with the Agriculture Select Committee (a major time-sapper itself) last week that I got my first whiff of corrupting influences.

I was with fellow members in the sleepy and antiseptic city of Brussels to discuss Common Agricultural Policy reform and fishing matters with a variety of individuals and bodies.

We were in the lift of the main European Commission building. I was observing other members struggling to dredge up from ill remembered snatches of school French to impress our Belgian guide when I looked up to notice the roll call of Euro Commissioners who had resigned en bloc, in some shame, months ago.[1]

"A pile of dead meat 'mongst that lot, I would have thought," said I, bringing their stilted Franglais to an unceremonious halt. But I was probably wrong.

Although its former President—Jacques Santer—has only very recently been replaced—with Romano Prodi—the rest of them remain, including Edith Cresson who was allegedly caught with her hand in the till of personal favours.

In Britain there would be an immediate packing of bags and a televised tearful departure. But in Brussels the Commissioners continue to have personal chauffeurs, a comfortable salary and generous allowances.

Having resigned they have all been back drawing their salaries and are unlikely to be replaced until at least September.

This is the best of both worlds—the same salary and perks but none of the burdensome responsibilities. I saw some of them shuffling around corridors, unavailable for meetings.

FOLLOWING the completion of devolution to Wales, Scotland and Northern Ireland a question will dawn on Cornwall…

Will Cornwall rise again or will we be sucked into a bland and pointless region with no identity?

With the Euro elections now upon us I am pleased that I can say that I opposed the nonsense of having a constituency which starts at the Isles of Scilly and the rugged Cornish coast and ends somewhere within the comfortable London commuter belt.

I know that, as a Liberal Democrat, I should be ecstatic about the introduction of the much loved proportional representation, but not in this form.

The certainty that the majority of electors will be mesmerised by the ballot paper on 10th June and unimpressed by seven MEPs all racing to be first on the scene of disasters, or glitzy good news stories after it, is reassuring to me and my admittedly Luddite views.[2]

Hopefully this will kill off any remaining hopes for the handful of supporters of a south west regional assembly—which has precisely zero popular support behind it.

Instead, it is time for Cornwall to stand up for itself and make the case for modest devolution to an Assembly of its own, before it is too late and Cornwall is abolished altogether by those who simply want to create a sanitised nowhere for bureaucratic convenience.

11th May 1999

[1]   In March 1999 the entire European Commission, led by Jacques Santer, the Commission President, resigned following a damning report on corruption and nepotism inside the Brussels Executive.

[2]   The turn out on 10th June 1999 meant that only one in four people participated in the 1999 elections to the European Parliament; the lowest figure for a UK-wide election. The Labour heartlands of the North of England showed a turnout below 20%.

Andrew George and Paddy Ashdown in Coinagehall Street, Helston 1997.

Padding around with election fever

WITH ELECTIONS over today, the Commons will now resume politics as usual.

But as phalanxes of battle-worn MPs come back from the front line to resume their seats, those on the Liberal Democrat benches will be girding their loins and taking up positions for another war of words—but this time with each other, when the Party Leadership election campaign commences.

The question on the minds of most observers of this spectator sport is whether a party crammed full of notoriously nice people can actually be beastly to each other.

Of course, all camps will be seeking the anointment of the outgoing leader, Paddy Ashdown, and it is perhaps worth dwelling for a moment on the momentous impact Paddy has made since becoming Liberal Democrat Leader nearly 12 years ago.

The Party came fourth in the first national elections (the 1989 Euros) at the beginning of his leadership. If there had been five national parties, I suspect that we would have come fifth!

PADDY is renowned within the Party for having taken a morning run, read all the newspapers, dictated all his memos for the day and pre-recorded two or three breakfast time interviews for television and radio before terrorising his staff and closest confidants with a bright and breezy "wake up" call of demands before 7.15 am.

I have occasionally met him in the House of Commons gym either during or after he has just hammered the hell out of unsuspecting gym equipment—which usually has "out of order" signs placed on it soon after he has finished.

When Paddy announced in January, his intention to stand down as Leader of the Party, his explanation sounded very much in character. It had all been decided years ago and was part of a life plan pre-determined by Paddy with characteristic military precision when he commenced his career with the Royal Marines, the Special Boat Service, the Diplomatic Service, etc. The rest is history.

The worst of all worlds for Paddy now would be if he were patronised with a gong, a boot "upstairs" to become "Lord Ashdown of Early Risings" and "put out to grass" on cosy un-demanding commissions to oversee national gardens or ancient memorials.

I cannot see Paddy retiring and I doubt that either the Prime Minister nor the Liberal Democrats would let him.

I was invited to dinner at Paddy & Jane Ashdown's modest London home recently when I suggested that when he joins me on the back benches he might like to take on an insignificant domestic portfolio and leave me to stride the world stage of international relations, diplomacy and combat resolution.

Of course, this is the very role for Paddy. It is on the international stage that Paddy's talents could unquestionably be employed to very great effect for the country.

Charles Kennedy, whom I support in the Leadership campaign[1], once described what he thought he heard on Paddy's answering machine, "please leave a message after the high moral tone". Even Paddy laughed at this.

However, being criticised for occasionally sounding sanctimonious in radio and television interviews did become a recurring theme. The truth is that Paddy is completely the opposite. Self-effacing, witty, quick-witted and very approachable and very different to the personality he sometimes puts across on more formal and public occasions.

Whoever we choose as our future Leader, we clearly will not be having a Leader in the mould of Paddy Ashdown. He has been a "one-off" and his tremendous record really speaks for itself.

I WAS PLEASANTLY surprised to have won an MPs' painting competition after turning up to smother a previously happy blank sheet of paper with a variety of Picasso-esque squiggles at a local playgroup. It was all in a very good cause. Drawing attention to the importance of the excellent work and services provided by the Pre-School Learning Alliance and the many hundreds of playgroups operating in Cornwall and elsewhere.

Because I had a prior appointment with a Home Office Minister on an obscure issue I was unable to attend a "paint-off" between Ken Clarke (for the Tories) and Barbara Follett (for Labour) in the Commons Dining Room. A delighted Matthew Taylor deputised in my absence.

As I fulfilled my obligation with a Minister, what appeared to be the whole of the world's media descended on the Commons Dining Room with reports on prime time national television as the three sharpened their paintbrushes for the finale. As I was unable to be there we can only guess at what "might have been". In the event Ken Clarke won by about a furlong.

What I learnt in the process was that the little cherubs who produce masterpieces at the age of 3—in the almost impossible circumstances of a limited number of primary poster colours, no time and absolute mayhem going on around them are clearly artistic geniuses whose talent should be appreciated more!

7th June 1999

[1]   *Charles Kennedy was elected Leader of the Liberal Democrats on 9th August 1999. The ballot went to four rounds before Mr Kennedy emerged a comfortable winner over Simon Hughes, by 28,425 votes (56.6%) to 21,833 (43.4%).*
David Rendel was the first of the five candidates to be eliminated, followed by Jackie Ballard and then Malcolm Bruce.

Learning from others

I HAVE just returned from a forty-eight hour tour to Iceland with a Select Committee looking at their fishing industry. And before you all sigh with cynicism and cry "nice work if you can get it", I must assure you that solitary confinement in Wormwood Scrubs would be infinitely preferable to a week on a tropical beach if accompanied by my dear colleagues on the Select Committee.

As I come from a part of the country well used to welcoming visitors, I know well the meaning of the long and patient look a native can give when presented with another specimen of tourist who displays the tell-tale sighs of loud, brash self-confidence in their own self-importance.

Dylan Thomas (who was married at St John's Hall, Penzance to Caitlin, so I feel I can quote him) once described one type of Englishman abroad as having "elephantiasis of the reputation".[1]

I have to admit to feeling like one of those teenagers you often see who appear to have been forced to go on holiday with their parents—and who always walk at least 20 yards behind, trying not to be seen with them. I tried blending in with the wonderful Icelandic people at every opportunity. But my failure to speak their language and their universal proficiency at mine gave the game away.

I have said before that it is a modern myth that "travel broadens the mind". The most ardent advocates seem to come back with the same teeny weeny little minds they went off with in the first place. And whilst we undoubtedly learnt an invaluable amount about the very impressive way the Icelanders manage their fisheries, I'm sure we ended up with an enhanced respect for the people there.

The fact is that with a population (270,000) little more than half that of Cornwall (nearly 500,000), this little nation, which finally secured independence from Denmark in 1944, can certainly teach us a thing or two. Despite an obviously hostile climate, Iceland has one of the highest life expectancies in the world. Indeed, though it has no defence budget or force, it successfully runs all state functions and has become an immensely wealthy nation. It is likely to join the EU in the next ten years and plays a significant humanitarian role with NATO and the UN.

Those who have experienced nothing but a dismissive scorn when suggesting that Cornwall and Scilly ought to have its own Regional Assembly should point their critics at the success story that is Iceland.

THE RECENTLY elevated Ann Widdecombe (now Tory Shadow Home Secretary) tiptoed to the despatch box for the first time this week.

She never was a person to cross lightly. I discovered this before the last General Election when she displayed a disturbingly detached indifference to the plight of a would-be deportee and his Cornish family I was helping three years ago. She was then a Home Office Minister. On this occasion we won. She found common cause with her more senior colleague—the then Home Secretary, Michael Howard.

Since then, having met the formidable woman, who is acknowledged as one of the Commons' more effective performers, it is quite clear that you wouldn't want her to trample on you.

However, with her characteristic disciplinarian matron of a girls' prep school manner, Widdecombe notoriously destroyed the leadership prospects of her colleague Michael Howard with the memorable claim that he "has something of the night about him".[2] I remember thinking with others in the chamber that if this were true then there was "something of the morning-after-the-night-before" about her.

Either way, it was clear that if this was how she treated her political friends, God help her enemies. I imagine Jack Straw must be taking self-defence lessons by now.

22nd June 1999

[1]   *Dylan Thomas, "A Visit to America" in Quite Early One Morning, 1954, p. 2.*
[2]   *In a strong personal attack on the former Home Office Minister first reported in the Sunday Times of 11th May 1997, Ann Widdecombe, who served under Michael Howard, described him as "dangerous", and said "He has something of the night about him". The comment was widely thought to have destroyed Howard's chance of standing for Conservative Party Leader.*

All-consuming committee leaves food for thought

I HAD MANAGED to avoid it until now, through skilfully avoiding eye contact at key moments, strategic absences and reassurance that my Select Committee was in the thick of a tortuous Inquiry.

But this week the inevitable happened. I had been put on a Standing Committee to take part in the weeks-on-end, morning and evening, line-by-line scrutiny of a Government Bill.

Short, one-off Standing Committees to check the correctness of allowing Ministers to get away with 'delegated' legislation on relatively minor matters have been regular and numerous for me. But sustained commitment to a Bill for two full days a week on top of my other responsibilities was going to be difficult to plan for.

In fact, the Bill I was asked to scrutinise was one which I've followed with relatively close interest—the Food Standards Bill. So in many ways, I was looking forward to the opportunity to bring forward amendments

Pictured by Peter Luff, fellow member of the Select Committee during a visit to a fish processing plant near Reykjavik, June 1999.

and challenge aspects of Government policy —particularly in the way the legislation would affect small food producers and retailers.

The primary purpose of the Bill is to set up a relatively autonomous Food Standards Agency—which now has all Party support.

I and others had challenged the Government not to charge all producers, manufacturers and retailers a flat rate charge of £90 a year towards the running of the Agency[1] as this would discriminate against small business. The lobbying worked and the Government dropped that proposal—but there still remained much to improve in the Bill.

HOWEVER, the first session of the Standing Committee was one of my most horrifying Parliamentary experiences. It was like jumping out of the normal work-a-day world of 'cut and thrust' and stumbling upon a timeless and never ending convention of train spotters.

The Committee is made up of 21 members, including Ministers, and appointed to reflect Party balance in the House. With two sittings on a Tuesday and two on a Thursday we hope to be through before the Summer recess—though, at the present rate, I doubt it.

I have put down a large number of amendments—mainly on matters of public interest and accountability and also to protect the interests of small business.

The 12 Government backbench members are the winners. All that is required of them by the Whips is their constant attendance and dutiful voting. They can productively fill their time by opening the mail, writing replies, reading reports and catching up on sleep, while I and other opposition MPs slug it out with the Ministers.

The process does become pretty futile, though. Anodyne and sensible rewordings are rejected by Ministers. They see it as their task to come out from the Committee with the Bill totally unscathed. They achieve this, not through rational debate but through numerical advantage.

This system has produced such "classics" as the Child Support Agency and the wrecking of the State Earnings Related Pension Scheme which robbed millions.

If, after weeks on end of banging my head against the brick wall of Government resolve, there appears a chink of light which accepts a reasoned amendment, then I will let you know.

Don't hold your breath.

6th July 1999

[1]   *The Government's proposal to introduce a controversial £90 flat fee on shops and restaurants to pay for the new Food Safety watchdog was abandoned in June 1999 after strong opposition from a cross-party committee of MPs and also from small retailers. They criticised the plans to charge small retailers the same as supermarkets. In a report on the draft Food Standards bill, the Agricultural Select Committee said the Government should instead implement a sliding scale of payment.*

"School's out"

I **USED** this column last year to issue certain death sentences upon anyone who dared to ask when my "long summer holiday" begins. It wasn't a wise thing to do. Happy constituents, hardly able to contain a satisfied smile, were provoked into what should have been kamikaze questions.

Therefore, this year, as we prepare for the summer recess from Parliament (but not from our constituency commitments!) I've decided to take it all on the chin—like hard working teachers.

In many ways it will provide an opportunity to bring a little sanity back to life. I won't miss leaving the Commons at 2 or 3 in the morning after late votes, only to be back again at 8 am to prepare for the first meeting; I won't miss knowing that there is nothing on earth that can stop the tedium of the repetition of an argument that most MPs would have heard so often they could repeat the words in their sleep, and I won't miss the use of outdated Parliamentary procedures to frustrate the progress of business.

It was on the last point that a former Fisheries Minister and I came to the Commons equivalent of "blows" this week.

I HAD "prayed" against a Government plan to impose new hygiene charges on our fishermen. Government Ministers had agreed—grudgingly—to set up a Parliamentary Standing Committee to debate my concerns. But a simple tactic of shouting "object" to the Parliamentary Business motions at the end of each day stopped it dead. So long as former minister Douglas Hogg used this Parliamentary procedure my concerns could not be debated.

This objection was not, as I later discovered when I accosted the MP, because he had a technical objection to my arguments or objected to the fishing industry's complaints. No. It had nothing at all to do with fish.

He had objected because he wanted to use any mechanism available to protest about the Government's policy on country blood sports.

These antics have been used for years to ensure that one or two maverick MPs can frustrate the clear will of the majority. A number of perfectly good Private Member's Bills—which had All Party support—have bitten the dust for this same reason. On many occasions the Bill would have had the support of the industry it was aimed at, no one objected, but a maverick MP had a grudge to settle and was prepared to sacrifice all that goodwill and weeks on end of careful parliamentary scrutiny to make their point.

Although I eventually won my right to set up the Standing Committee I have to say I could do with a few weeks away from this madness to recover my sanity, what is left of it.

BUT I WILL miss the Commons Tea Room. It is a friendly retreat when lunacy is breaking out everywhere else.

It operates like a school Common Room. Gangs congregate in unspoken territories—though many break ranks and mix with other parties.

Most come in for morale-boosting sustenance and something to eat and drink. But although it is the tittle-tattle epicentre of the Commons, Whips equipped with bionic hearing are known to loiter. So care is always taken and the conversations remain happy and light.

20th July 1999

Ambitious to avoid failure

IF **"HAPPINESS** is keeping as small a space as possible between hope and achievement"[1] then there would be very little disappointment amongst Government Back Benchers this week.

I didn't detect that future Prime Ministers were waiting by their pagers in anticipation of the call-up in the hope of taking red boxes away with them before they sunned themselves in Tuscany.

The widely trailed and dramatic shift in the make up of the Government Cabinet which never happened turned out to be a pre-silly season storm in a teacup.[2]

After all of the speculation, it was the deft move of the smooth Desmond Lynam from one channel to another which caused the biggest shock.[3]

The belief that all political careers end in failure is based on the myth that all MPs hope to become Prime Minister. And though many MPs may allow their ambitions to "develop" during their careers, it is my impression that most ambitions remain personally realistic and modest, but for their constituents and constituency considerably more ambitious.

The biggest political failure of all, in fact, is amongst those politicians who allow personal ambition to override the ambitions they should have for the constituency which elected them.

MANY of my Parliamentary colleagues will be coming to West Cornwall and the Isles of Scilly for their holidays. This will include a number of Ministers who will be in the area for the Eclipse. They are, of course, welcome to the paradise that is my constituency and to meet the paragons of rectitude and virtue who are my constituents.

I am hoping to meet up with some of them while they are down, on the strict proviso that they prostrate themselves before my constituents and confess their envy. For those MPs who can't make it I have requested them to send "wish I was there" postcards.

As we don't get our fair share of the national wealth, I see no reason why we shouldn't, at this time of year, receive more than our fair share of national appreciation.

If you have the opportunity to do so, have a good holiday.

3rd August 1999

[1] Paul Flynn, Labour member for Newport West in Commons Knowledge: How to be a Backbencher, 1997, p.148.
[2] After intense speculation about a Cabinet reshuffle Blair made just one Cabinet change at the end of July 1999.
[3] Des Lynam, the BBC's sports anchorman left the Corporation after thirty years in August 1999 to become ITV's main football presenter.

Politicians should let fishermen reclaim their industry

THERE ARE AT LEAST two inevitable outcomes when a politician chooses to pop his head above the parapet to express a view on the fishing industry.

The first is, of course, that the usual handful of obsessed Europhobes are provoked onto their high horses and proceed to fire off a volley of missives in all directions.

The second is that the media will wheel out a handful of angry fishermen to let the politician know just how ridiculously out of touch he really is.

The result is usually a kind of fudged stalemate. So, until the next unwary politician—perhaps inadvertently—stumbles upon this lair, it remains a political "NO WIN AREA" and is avoided in preference to issues where spin doctors can exert more control.

And that's the problem. Fishing policy has become piecemeal and reactive. Politicians—because they always rush for the political sunlit uplands of Health, Education and Law and Order—generally don't understand the fishermen's problems and fishermen don't understand the problems which politicians have with the fishing industry.

Politicians generally hope to rush in and out quickly before they're either dragged down the side alley of Europhobia or are lynched merely for being a politician.

If you were seeking to contrive a position from which to establish really bad fishing policy, you couldn't do a lot better than to start from this position.

I SUPPOSE I can be frank about both fishermen and politicians because I know them both pretty well equally now. Though before I was elected to become MP for West Cornwall and Scilly two years ago I have to admit that I knew fishermen a great deal better.

After all I was born and brought up in a fishing village on The Lizard. My ancestors were (and now many family and friends are) still engaged in the industry.

That's why I was particularly keen that the Agriculture Select Committee—of which I am a member—should undertake an inquiry into the state of the British fishing industry.

On inflatable during 2 day visit to fisheries protection vessel HMS Anglesea.

Now the Select Committee has reported[1], following what has involved the best part of a year looking into the industry and including visits to Newlyn, Grimsby, Brussels, Spain, Shetland, Billingsgate and Iceland. The All Party Committee came to remarkable consensus on the key areas, with even the former Tory Fishing Minister and Europhile, David Curry MP, and Europhobic Labour MP, Austin Mitchell, finding many areas of common ground with me.

Clearly, no one can criticise the Government for not spending a high proportion of public finance on the fishing industry. Some £108 million of public money every year is spent on enforcement, research, scientific support, fisheries grants, the Maritime and Coastguard Agency and other administrative tasks. Of this, expenditure directly attributable to the UK catching sector alone equates to approximately 7% of the value of the fishing industry, but a much higher proportion of the value of the catch.

Despite this level of public finance, the fishing industry in the UK has done well in presenting itself as suffering from political neglect or mistreatment over the years.

Either way, the UK fishing industry is seen—in comparison to its competitors on the continent, in Norway and Iceland—as failing.

DURING the Inquiry, I asked a fishermen's leader in Spain what he felt were the most significant ingredients of a successful fishing industry. His simple reply outlined the three essentials. You need "fish, a means of catching it and you need a market".

And, put simply, that's what our Inquiry sought to deal with. How to ensure there is a healthy stock of fish in the sea; how to relate the catching capacity to the available fish and how to ensure that the full value of the fish caught is appreciated in the market.

What the Inquiry Report recommends is that we need an overall vision and strategy for the fishing industry which allows the development of the industry in all three areas.

First, there was little question that, in those countries where the fishing industry has been successful, the relationship between fishermen and scientists is good and constructive. The recent history of the Grand Banks off the Canadian East coast should teach us that.

The report recommends a much clearer collaborative structure for fishermen and scientists, rather than the eleventh hour "facing down" process which seems to happen on an annual basis. This will require considerable "give" on both sides but I am certain that scientists themselves must recognise that a great deal more knowledge and experience is held by fishermen than is appreciated and that much of the "pure" research undertaken needs to be translated into practical and "applied" knowledge.

Second, the Select Committee saw the need for an updating of the powers of Sea Fisheries Committees; encouragement for fishermen to be given greater responsibility for the management of their fisheries; a clear Government policy to deal with the transferability and market value of fishing quotas and the need to demonstrate that there really is an even playing field in management mechanisms and enforcement regimes throughout Europe.

Finally, the Committee recommends the modernisation of marketing mechanisms. Clearly, sea fish is the most healthy, animal friendly and arguably the most tasty source of protein available to us but has been seen for too long as "poor man's meat". Most of the fish we eat in this country has to be boneless, skinless, shapeless and bland and a great deal more needs to be done to develop the market.

OVERALL the Select Committee believes that it is now time for the Government to establish a clear vision and long term fishing policy. It should allow fishermen to reclaim ownership of the management of the industry; an effective and collaborative relationship between scientists and fishermen; a mechanism to protect vulnerable fishing communities like those around the coast of Cornwall and an opportunity to invest in proper marketing and market structures.

The best thing for both politicians and fishermen would be if politicians could leave fishermen to largely manage their own industry themselves. That's what we should be moving towards. We should be able to take overbearing Government largely out of the equation. This way politicians and fishermen can happily co-exist.

Written for the Western Morning News and Fishing News

9th August 1999

[1] Agriculture Select Committee's Eighth Report—Sea Fishing—published 27th July 1999

More 'bucket-and-spade' than 'castles-in-the-air'

THE PUBLIC may be under the impression that all MPs decamp to the Mediterranean to choose a beach to be cleared as their private fiefdom during the month of August.

I am sure that the prospect of the U.K. Prime Minister seeking someone to "share a thought" with is enough to clear the locals from any Italian beach[1].

On the other hand, I know that many of us have been diligently operating on the home front, attempting to keep the mountains of constituency casework under control and to prepare for the Autumn's harvest of new Parliamentary Bills. (We have also had to endure the penance of the "Prescott/Widdecombe Show" as they both play at Prime Minister and Tory Leader while the boss is away.)

Meanwhile, some MPs succumb to the temptation of accepting free or subsidised trips to faraway places. Some visits are good value for taxpayers' and other people's money. Occasional visits by those with specialist knowledge of a country or as election observers are worthwhile, particularly and most recently, in East Timor.[2]

MPs do recognise the "travel gluttons" amongst their colleagues who need to be regularly consoled by long hours in the sun at a pool side of a luxury hotel. Often the hospitality is laid on by "Mega-Greed plc", an oppressive regime or environmental polluters.

However, for many MPs the time to catch up and reorganise is occasionally punctuated by the pleasures of a break to engage in "trolley rage" in the local shops or, more preferably, territory reclamation on a local beach.

NOW THAT the PM is returning from his holiday, attention may turn to the battle ground for the autumn. Yet one matter which is unlikely to be debated in the House of Commons is how the Chancellor of the Exchequer will spend the rapidly accumulating "general election war chest" being created by the ongoing planned budget surplus.

I suspect that the strategy is to wait until the Spring of 2001 to go on a spending spree to please voters assumed to have terminally short memories. When our farmers, our teachers, our doctors and nurses are all struggling with what are, hopefully, short term problems now, the promise of "jam tomorrow" is a little like reassuring constituents in Cornwall that the Millennium Dome will have an economic "knock-on" effect outside the South East of England.

NEWS LAST WEEK that we Liberal Democrat MPs are being asked by new Leader Charles Kennedy to write our own job description has brought on speculation that there will be 46 erstwhile Shadow Ministers for Constitutional Affairs. The belief that the Party is only interested in rarefied debate on questions of "process" is much exaggerated!

For my part, I hope that all other MPs will compete to become the most respected Constitution Anorak in the Parliamentary Party, which may leave some substantial vacancies. Meanwhile, I remain tight lipped.

31st August 1999

[1]   *A row erupted when it emerged that the beach near the Blair's Tuscany holiday home, normally open to the public, was to be closed during the Blair family's visit. Tony Blair attempted to defuse the controversy by asking the Italian police to reopen the 5km stretch.*

[2]   *On 30th August 1999 the people of East Timor voted to reject Indonesian rule. The United Nations sponsored ballot brought to an end a period of brutal occupation. The Indonesian army unleashed a systematic campaign of terror in an attempt to influence the vote.*

Next...world domination

CONFERENCE SEASON is upon us again. Rash claims, demonising the opposition and sending supporters back to constituencies to prepare for world domination are the stock in trade.

Yet, despite all of the strange tub thumping and extravagant claims, Conferences can inspire your troops and fringe meetings can help to expose party divisions in a frank and entertaining way.

The auditorium is ringed by compassionate charities, environmental campaign groups and their tormentors from "Mega-Greed Inc" and "Souls-sold-to-the-Devil Alliances"—all in close proximity to each other. When the Conference is in full swing their reps exchange cheesy smiles to each other.

The Liberal Democrats have been in Harrogate this week and MPs have had to get used to the disconcerting experience of not always being the centre of attention. The new egos on the block are Scottish Parliamentarians, Welsh "Assemblians", a big crop of Euro MPs and now four Government Ministers—in our case from the Scottish Parliament.

Cynics who have effectively argued that any Party's priorities go through dramatic modification when they have to face the reality of implementing policy in the cold light of day, have been surprised that the transition in Scotland—despite headlines of the party "caving in" at the time—has been relatively smooth. Even on the matter of scrapping student tuition fees the party remains quietly confident of ultimately achieving its objective in Scotland.[1]

NORMAL political processes continue unabated even though the Westminster Parliament is still not sitting. Party Conferences provide the first opportunity for the old cosy cabal of politicians and media to exert some pressure on Government Ministers after the August "slow down".

Indeed, speaking at a National Farmers' Union Meeting this week, only one hour after the announcement of a half billion pound support package for the farming industry[2]—though most of it was recycled "old" money—I was able to take some credit. Whether the Minister was indeed "terrified of the savaging we would give the

Government" for failing to properly respond to the true extent of the crisis in farming or it was the result of recent meetings with our representatives and the planned farmers protest at next week's Labour Conference in Bournemouth, we can only speculate. Either way the political process is now back in full swing.

Time to dust off your campaign plans for the autumn and give them a whirl.

20th September 1999

[1]   *Because Labour had no overall majority in the new Scottish Parliament an Executive Coalition was established with Scottish Liberal Democrat Leader Jim Wallace becoming Deputy First Minister to Labour's Donald Dewar. On 25th January 2000, after increasing pressure from the Liberal Democrat members on the Scottish Executive tuition fees were abolished in Scottish Universities from Autumn 2000.*
[2]   *The then Agriculture Minister, Nick Brown, announced an aid package for Britain's livestock farmers hit by the crisis over mad cow disease and a slump in the market for lamb. The package was worth around £0.5bn, two-thirds of which came from the European Union.*

Conference season: The booby traps are set...

LIFE CAN be so unfair.

You go to your own Party Conference believing that the stage has been set for you, but little did you know or has any one warned you that in fact it has also been booby trapped.

After all, picture this. You accept a short lift—a mere 300 yards—to avoid wind and rain, before your key note Labour Conference speech, about which you are understandably anxious. The journalists reporting it are driven there too, but they're more interested in your mode of transport than in what you have to say.[1]

Or suppose you are about to lift the spirits of the Conservative faithful with a speech extolling all that is good about their Party (a necessarily short speech, but a speech nevertheless), but you find that the publishers of two biographies have cleverly stolen the limelight.[2]

It is not that we politicians are hell bent on self-destruction. Though we can sometimes be drawn into a false sense of security at our Party Conference that the whole event is our "shop window" to the world and that, therefore, nothing can go wrong.

Examples of how things can go wrong seem to more than justify why a "once bitten twice shy" politician might call upon the services of a "spin doctor" to attempt to foresee and manage these carefully set booby traps.[3]

WILLIAM Randolph Hearst once described news as "something, someone, somewhere doesn't want to see published—everything else is advertising". But this "investigate and expose" view of life can generate its own feeding frenzy, and can itself be cleverly exploited by an experienced spin doctor.

A fellow MP explained to me that "you have to remember that tabloid journalists are reared in special veal crates in an alien land in order to develop their sub-human view of the instincts of their readers and listeners".[4]

Alternatively, others believe that all journalists—with, of course, the honourable exception of local journos in Cornwall—are those unreformable school bullies who naturally gravitate towards the profession because it gives them a chance of picking on people in public life to demonstrate the slightest frailty or weakness and can operate in the almost certain knowledge that there is little chance of retaliation.

Seeing how politicians react to all of this taunting and bullying can be fascinating. It is certainly true that trivialising a sub plot can knock a politician off course from the main purpose. Each time it happens, headlines are briefly grabbed, newspapers sold and politicians become a little more cynical.

What people have to remember is that all politicians were themselves human beings once, before they chose or were catapulted into this strange existence. Many of us still have almost humanising flash backs of what it is like to be normal, but usually survive the experience to carry on impervious to the world around!

SECOND home ownership has hit the headlines again. Environment Minister, Michael Meacher, believes that second home ownership should be controlled in those areas where local people cannot find adequate housing.

To me, this statement came as a welcome surprise. I had challenged the Government on the inequity of the previous Government's legacy which leaves poor locals in mobile homes and poor standard accommodation having to pay more council tax than second home owners who get a discount! The Minister then refused to act.[5]

I do not believe that second homers are themselves wicked. It is the system—which allows large numbers of Cornish and Scillonian properties to be used for private recreation rather than meeting a large and unmet local need—which needs changing.

I remember the last time I raised my concerns with the Government I received a flurry of sometimes hostile letters from second homers who wrote to criticise my actions. At the same time my casework surgeries were packed with many local people queuing up with cases of desperate housing need and for reasons not of their own making.

The situation is clearly unacceptable. Something needs to be done. But using it as an excuse to generate a fresh "class war" will not be the answer.

5th October 1999

[1] John Prescott, Deputy Prime Minister and Minister for Transport, was widely criticised after being driven 250 yards to speak out against car use at the Labour Party Conference.

[2] John Major: The Autobiography and In Office, the memoirs of former Chancellor, Norman Lamont, were both published in October 1999. They were seen as reopening divisions in the Conservative Party.

[3] American newspaper publisher and tycoon (1863-1951). He sensationalised journalism by the introduction of banner headlines and lavish illustrations. Believed by many to have initiated the Spanish-American War of 1898 to encourage sales of his newspaper, he also advocated political assassination in editorial just months before the assassination of President McKinley. A member of the US House of Representatives (1903-07), he failed in his attempts to become Mayor and Governor of New York. His life inspired the Orson Welles' film Citizen Kane.

[4] Paul Flynn, Labour member for Newport West.

[5] However, Andrew George, raised further questions with Environment Minister Chris Mullin MP on 9th February 2000, when progress was eventually made which resulted in a policy change incorporated in proposals in the Government's Rural Areas White Paper in November 2000.

Democracy in action

THOSE WHO have survived unscathed after asking me when the "MP's holiday" is over will be interested to know that Parliamentary recess ended this week. We have all now filed back into the Commons for another session of cut and thrust.

Hard-working MPs have now returned from a punishing schedule of months of constituency casework meetings and visits, to take up local matters with Government Ministers.

And in preparation for the Commons Chamber, many have rehearsed the "arts" of politics. I am sure that many practice being outraged and limber up for a new season of green bench hooliganism.

Those who have sharpened the sound bites, rehearsed the awful puns and spent time revising the arts of the economies of truth will have an edge on the rest.

But it is also a time when an MP changes mode. From taking more time to get down to look at a subject in more detail—farm visits, spending a day at sea, wall to wall constituency meetings—to talking on more, but at the risk of not having the time to be familiar with the subject.

After all, in Parliament this week, I will raise matters over fishing safety grants, follow through my query to the Home Secretary on Police numbers in Cornwall, ask the Health Secretary about NHS dentistry in Cornwall, attend two Select Committee sessions to investigate the marketing of milk, meet the project manager for Hayle Harbour, discuss pensions issues, deliver a demand to the PM on Objective One funding matters, speak at a meeting on rural anti-racism (a project of which I am a trustee) attend briefings or meetings on Europe, wildlife protection and bereavement counselling, have project meetings with the World Wildlife Fund for Nature on inshore fishing and with other MPs on disability benefits, prepare plans to tackle problems on hospital waiting times and question the Attorney General on the outcome of the Glidewell Report into the Crown Prosecution Service and much, much more. And this in the three days I'm in London this week.

No wonder I describe the MP's lot as "Jack of all trades—master of none".

However, some MPs are better able to disguise their failure to master all subjects than others!

AS WE RETURN in a celebration of democracy we are presented with an odd vision of democracy turned upside down in Pakistan.

The evening the news broke of General Musharraf's bloodless coup, I spoke to a good friend from Pakistan who works here. Expecting outrage, panic and fear I was surprised to hear a mix of calm anticipation and a sense of assurance which bordered on optimism. Since then, the clear impression of a country at ease with having their apparently democratically elected President and Government deposed and replaced with a military regime has created great soul searching amongst western democracies.[1]

Perhaps it's a case of "better the devil you don't know, than the devil you know".

Things will have come to a pretty pass here when a country like the U.K. reacts as Pakistan has. We are used to negative campaigning—especially at election time—and the motivation to vote against something or someone is more often greater than an enthusiasm to vote in favour or in support.

Serious question marks over the purpose of democracy—if it doesn't represent the "popular will"—and of the effect of negative campaigning will be at stake as the international community—I hope—seek to offer support to Pakistan in what we hope will be a transition to effective properly accountable and democratic government.

19th October 1999

[1]   On 12th October 1999 General Pervez Musharraf led a successful coup against the Pakistani Government of Nawaz Sharif, Leader of the Muslim League party.

The natives are revolting on the benches

A **QUIET REVOLUTION** is taking place in the publicity hungry environment of Parliament.

By the time tens of thousands of avid *Cornishman* readers have sprinted down to the newsagent first thing on Thursday morning to pick up this copy, in customary eager anticipation, the first evidence of this new phenomenon will be known.

Because "re-selection" has been an uncomfortable word when uttered in the unattributable torture chamber of a Party Whip's office—especially that of the Governing party. But, while "spin doctors" have been spinning and weaving their version of the truth to their hearts' content and "control freaks" have taken no more than the usual sadistic pleasure in dangling the thumb screws over any Government backbencher who dares to show independence of thought or (worse) deed, MPs of conscience have been quietly and efficiently organising their own reselection for the next general election.

Thus, some of the most uncontrol-freakable backbenchers have become immune to the ultimate sanction for "wrong doing"—i.e. DE-selection.

Indeed, a friend on the Agriculture Select Committee—Austin Mitchell (Grimsby)—writing recently about his own reselection process claims that he is "playing safe: praising the Leader, defending Party policies wherever he can find them and explaining that money allocated 17 times before is still new money".[1]

THE REASON I'm telling you all this is because we face the outside prospect of a possible Government defeat in the Commons on a key plank of its Welfare Reform. However, it will be late on Wednesday night or early Thursday morning; not early enough for me confidently to predict the outcome and too late to have any chance of being accurately reported in the morning newspapers.[2]

The context for me is that our new Leader, Charles Kennedy, has honoured me with the opportunity of getting stuck into disability matters. This will give me an early chance to challenge the Government on its proposal to scrap Severe Disablement Allowance and tighten the rules on Incapacity Benefit.

In normal circumstances Lobby Journalists find social security matters mind-bogglingly dull.

More people are on Housing Benefit than have mortgages. Lobby journalists have mortgages. None have Housing Benefit. The complexities of contribution records, means testing and entitlement criteria are a far off, over the horizon jungle of incomprehension.

Even those who take an interest find it difficult to persuade their Editor that the plight of millions of people on the margins of society and with minute disposable incomes is of any importance. (Not so with the honourable Editor of *The Cornishman,* of course.)

However, tell those same Editors about a genuine prospect of a Government defeat and they suddenly prick up their ears.

But they do not have to overcome the North West face of Everest learning curve which I've been challenged with this week. For them it is purely a matter of parliamentary arithmetic and the numerical strength of the Labour backbench rebellion.

In what are, admittedly, "interesting times", politically I do hope that genuine concern over finding proper improvements in benefits for the severely disabled is not overlooked.

The Government has got it wrong here. The legislation needs improving. Many thousands of the most vulnerable—including hundreds in West Cornwall and on Scilly—would be impoverished by this and it is right that, as MPs of all parties, we should ask the Government to think again.

2nd November 1999

[1]   The House Magazine; the Parliamentary Weekly No. 871, Vol. 24, 1st November 1999
[2]   In the event, on 3rd November 1999, around 50 Labour MPs voted against two key clauses in the Welfare Reform and Pensions Bill. Not enough to overturn the Government's majority.

Tangled web leads to mock mayor

IF YOU believe that the House of Commons looks to the world like a side show then recent events would certainly appear to prove it.

I had stood in the frozen sunlight of College Green opposite the Lords doing verbal battle on Radio 5 "Live". The Queen arrived in impressive stagecoach and entourage, with the full splendour of the Household Guard to open the new session of the "Mother of Parliaments". She read her "Queen's Speech" to a recently humbled and hushed House of Lords.

Yet the Prime Minister at the height of his powers, with massive Parliamentary majority, supported by the massed ranks of "spin doctors" and "control freaks", had prepared a speech which set the place alight only with cigarette lighters as the hardened hacks of the Press Gallery valiantly struggled to stifle its collective yawn.

Perhaps the real action was happening somewhere else. Perhaps debating policy is really like drawing teeth and light relief is called for. Well there was plenty of that to come.

NOW, politics is full of hard bitten old cynics. The received wisdom sees truth as a commodity which is only dragged out of unwilling politicians when they finally run out of excuses and that all simple events are never what they seem but have a sinister motive.

If you introduce into this world the simple, happy and innocent truth of a Downing Street pregnancy then the conspiracy theorists will have a field day...[1]

Clearly (so it was seriously reasoned) the pregnancy was designed to helpfully deflect attention away from Labour's Mayoral selection fiasco. Or it was to soften the impact of the detailed scrutiny of the Queen's Speech. (Of course, all the time, I knew that it was because the PM couldn't answer my questions about the Government's contribution to Cornwall's Objective One programme!)[2]

Sadly, this view of the world is already anticipating that the baby's birth will be used as a perfect decoy to release quietly a policy announcement to reintroduce the Workhouse and news about the baby's first tooth will mask plans for further savage cuts in benefits for the disabled.

Innocence and childhood have no place in this tangled world. "O what a tangled web we weave, when…we practice to deceive"[3] and politicians should be masters at this.

MEANWHILE, my prize for "Spin of the week" has to go to the blessed Daily Telegraph leader writer who loyally offered London Conservatives "Congratulations", claiming that giving their members a renewed choice of candidate "contrasts favourably with Labour" and "will yield dividends when the election itself comes". Sounds like the England Test team claiming a moral victory in Johannesburg.[4]

In contrast Liberal Democrats could hardly contain their anger when it was revealed this week that they have selected a nice, squeaky clean business woman—Susan Kramer—who has incompetently failed to fall out with her Party leadership and, worse, who appears not to have a single skeleton in her closet! "All she can ever talk about is policy and London," one dejected London Lib Dem MP confided to me this week.

Needless to say, many in the London Party are demanding her de-selection and a re-contest for fear of being frozen out of the publicity limelight altogether.

Whenever we experience self doubt about our ability to take charge of our own affairs here in Cornwall, we can at least console ourselves that we couldn't look more ridiculous than the contest for the top job in Britain's revered capital city.

In these circumstances Penzance's own mock Mayor would look like a serious candidate.[5]

23rd November 1999

[1] *In November 1999 the Blairs announced that they were expecting their fourth child. Leo Blair was born on 20th May 2000.*

[2] *See Appendix, page 181.*

[3] *Sir Walter Scott—'The Lay of the Last Minstrel'*

[4] *The England Cricket Team toured South Africa in the winter of 1999/2000 losing the Series 2-1. By this stage in the tour, England had already been very heavily defeated.*

[5] *In what is a predictably hilarious event and after much local media speculation and intrigue, Penzance elects its own Mock Mayor during the Golowan Festival (in late June) in time for Mazey Day (a popular, colourful and raucous community gathering).*

Fishing for Christmas cards

IT'S THAT time of year. Amongst the tinsel, carols and nativity scenes in comes Parliament's annual fisheries debate. For the people of West Cornwall and the Isles of Scilly the debate is, of course, a matter of very critical importance. Christmas is always a tense and critical time for the fishing industry, because only two weeks from the commencement of the next fishing year the industry discovers what next year's quota will be.

This year is proving particularly crucial as the scientific assessment of stock levels points to the need for the biggest cuts in fishing quotas the industry has seen. For the main stocks targeted by the Newlyn fleet the proposed cuts will be very painful to bear. It could devastate Newlyn and would certainly undermine the economic viability of much of the fleet.

The debate was squeezed into just over two hours of parliamentary time which was a shockingly small period of time to give to a key industry and one in which men consistently risk their lives to put fish on our dinner tables.

Of course, as usual, there were those who wanted to use fishermen and the industry as a convenient battleground for their own anti European wars. But that really isn't the issue.

Sir Ted Heath—former Prime Minister—used the debate as a rare opportunity to speak from experience and to contradict the present Conservative position on Europe and fishing.

The real issue is how to manage the fish stocks as they swim around and between traditional territorial waters.

After all, the science may not be precise but we are encouraging fishermen and scientists to work together to improve what we know about fish, their life cycle and health.

However, although fish aren't very bright, we do at least know that they have brains just large enough not to have any hang ups about nationality.

The bottom line is that we shouldn't be in this position. The industry is unable to plan more than a year ahead and that's not good enough. The Common Fisheries Policy has been a shambles, stocks are not being managed well and quotas are constantly being cut as a result.

The challenge to us all is to radically reform the CFP to give more power to fishermen to manage their own stocks in partnership with scientists and environmentalists; and to prepare a plan for the fishing industry which allows it to look five and ten years ahead rather than just a few weeks.

CHRISTMAS IS a time of goodwill to all men and women but obviously not to politicians.

Someone came breathlessly up to me in the street at the weekend asking how I "put up with it!"

They were referring to the problem of constantly being made a convenient butt for criticism and blame and referred to an article in a local newspaper (not *The Cornishman*) which had celebrated an achievement I had secured for a local town with, I was told, snide and grudging remarks which had clearly shocked my constituent.

"Never lower yourself by responding." "Let the comments by others say more about them than it does about you", were the best responses I could muster.

But it is true, if you respond to all gratuitous abuse you could end up—as no doubt Stephen Norris is finding in London—by taking the drastic last resort step of actually removing people from your Christmas card list![1]

14th December 1999

[1]   On 11th December 1999 Steven Norris was deselected as the Conservative candidate for London Mayor. He blamed this on the decisions of a "blue-rinsed coven" of women led by Diane Collins, Chair of his Constituency, who was allegedly bitter about Norris's personal life after her own divorce. Norris was later reselected after the withdrawal of disgraced Lord Archer.

Cornwall: Are we being frogmarched (or merely sleepwalking) into extinction?

FOR ME IT was a brief trip to Iceland earlier this year which brought into sharp focus my growing concern about the slide of Cornwall over the precipice into extinction.

Icelandic people are proud and distinctive. Their pride and distinctiveness is the bedrock from which they can concentrate on their priorities and on success.

Since achieving independence from Denmark in 1944 this relatively poor island has become one of the wealthiest nations on earth. It has a higher Gross Domestic Product per person than not only the United Kingdom, but France, Germany and Japan as well. It has achieved low inflation and a high standard of living, the highest life expectancy of any nation in the world and enviable economic prospects for the future.

And all of this with a population of 270,000—little more than half that of Cornwall (approx 500,000).

CORNWALL should have learned lessons from this, if it hadn't been left by successive governments to drift aimlessly in the other direction.

I am not suggesting that Cornwall should declare independence— that would be absurd, unrealistic and patently unobtainable.

However, we in Cornwall might learn that through being clear about our own strengths, knowing what we want to achieve, standing up for ourselves and then going out there with a determination to succeed, we might be taking destiny by the scruff of the neck, instead of sleep-walking cap in hand into the next millennium.

But, perhaps it is now time to turn self doubt into self belief. Because from being honourably distinct, Cornwall now runs the risk of becoming indistinguishable. It also faces the paradox of being both one of the most distinctive regions in the UK, but with its services more merged with others than anywhere else.

Just look at the record of recent years. Not only has the Truro MAFF office moved to Exeter, and the Camborne Police Operations planned to be moved to Plymouth, but Cornwall's Careers Service, the Magistrates' Court Committee, and the Learning and Skills Council has merged with those in Devon.

Following this the Government has plans to merge Cornwall's Probation Service and there are fears that the Fire Service and the Health Authority will go the same way. And all of this after the Government dismissed Cornwall's claim for a Regional Development Agency of its own, despite Cornwall's very strong and eventually successful campaign to obtain separate European regional status for the purpose of obtaining Objective One funding. What next? Education, Social Services, Housing? This would leave Cornwall as a souped up Parish Council.

THE CONTRAST with Iceland could hardly be more stark. While a country with a population half that of Cornwall forges on relentlessly to greater and greater success, Cornwall can't even train our own 17- and 18-year olds, administer minor justice, advise our young people on their future careers, police ourselves, plan the development of our economy, organise support for our farming and fishing industries, nor for that matter a whole host of other subordinate services.

The conventional arguments against a place like Cornwall thinking, planning and acting for itself, even on these relatively insignificant matters, is that it is "too small"; that it hasn't got "the clout" in the corridors of power; and that it cannot achieve the "economies of scale".

But, as time goes on, these justifications ring more hollow. It is the modern day equivalent of the "Emperor's clothes". They are justifications which are repeated mantra fashion as the unquestioned and accepted wisdom of the day.

These mergers are bad news for Cornwall. Not only does the merging of services result in the removal of the higher paid jobs to the east, contributes to the loss of control over services, masks account-ability, results in more remote management but, above all, it actually cuts off the better option of Cornwall standing up for itself; with the more effective "clout" of its distinctiveness; a distinctiveness based as much on its size as upon the many other unique factors of Cornwall.

Of course, I am not saying that Cornwall should not co-operate with other areas on a project by project basis. The occasional liaison with other areas (whether Devon or elsewhere) can bring renewed vitality. But, an enforced marriage can kill off any lust to succeed and usually ends in tears and disappointment.

IF SUCCESSIVE governments are making intended or unintended decisions to gradually merge Cornwall into extinction, I think it is only right that we have an opportunity to debate this.

And those who have been reassured by the Government's present enthusiasm to devolve power from the centre might wish to reflect on how this has ended abruptly with devolution to Scotland, Wales and Northern Ireland in London. Because, with few exceptions, the Government's notion of "English" regions doesn't actually exist other than as bureaucratic constructs for administrative ease. There is no popular consensus.

Attempts to create a new identity or legitimacy for these regions won't wash with the majority.

It is not that I believe we should join the tiny handful of certifiable nationalists who want Cornwall to be "cut-off" from the rest of the world. Quite the opposite. It is time for Cornwall to cut itself *into* the action happening around Europe and elsewhere. Cornwall has a great deal to contribute to the celebration of diversity both within Britain and a wider world.

Cornwall does not need to accept passively the future lovingly mapped out for it. Cornwall has the choice of being determined to build on the success of its Objective One campaign or to allow Government "merger mania" to sleepwalk it into extinction.

It's time for Cornwall to rediscover its distinctiveness and self belief—creating a strong economy based on Cornwall's unique strength through distinctive branding, becoming the "Green Peninsula" of the UK, developing its unique potential in higher education, maritime development and new technologies. We can and should learn from others.

Western Morning News, 18th December 1999

Being bugged by the next Millennium

IF I WERE WRITING a New Millennium message for a national newspaper I suppose I would ponder whether democracy will survive, whether war, famine, disease or natural disaster will destroy human kind itself, in the next thousand years.

But assuming mankind survives and that something resembling accountability to ordinary folk continues in some form, the big question for us is whether a place like Cornwall—or like the Isles of Scilly for that matter—will exist in any meaningful sense of the word. Perhaps we only need to look at the celebration of the millennium itself to demonstrate just how much our self confidence is synthetic and our technical abilities are deeply fallible.

We are supposed to be celebrating Jesus Christ's 2000th birthday, but most who understand these things agree that the start of the new Millennium should in fact be around the 1st January 2001. Perhaps we could all have another big jamboree at the same time next year!

And the self confidence generated by the new age of information technology has been undermined by fear of the dear old Millennium Bug. How easily we're tripped up by bathing in our own glory.

As for Cornwall itself, we show all the signs at present of either being frogmarched or sleepwalking into extinction.

Does it matter? Is there anything about the place that is Cornwall that is worth preserving?

The question as to whether Cornwall, the Isles of Scilly and places like it will still exist as entities in a thousand years time is critical, in my view, to the democratic process. In a world which constantly seeks bureaucratic convenience and administrative ease, do "place", "identity", "community" and "cultural heritage" count for anything at all? I believe that they must and it should be a measure of the success of our political health that these factors are encouraged and promoted for the good, rather than abolished without proper consideration.

Now that Cornwall and Scilly have entered the new Millennium, the challenge is on and we must see whether the qualities of life they represent are factors which can be promoted and be a basis on which to build an effective political system for the next thousand years.

31st December 1999

Brand new century: Same old drivel

NEW YEAR, new century, new millennium. But the same old drivel emanates from the political establishment. There is, I suppose, one difference which seems to have its origins in the celebrations for the Millennium itself. That is that the "Midas" touch appears to have deserted the Prime Minister recently.

His Home Secretary has been hit with a spate of "no win" scenarios from the response to the deportation of accused former Nazi war criminal, Konrad Kalejs[1], the medical report on General Pinochet[2], the overlooking of normal procedure to allow Mike Tyson into the country[3], the reported rise in crime figures of 2.2%[4] and now the overwhelming defeat of the Government's proposals to remove the option of trial by jury for some defendants[5].

The truth is that while many of these bad news stories are the product of circumstances beyond Government's control, at least half are the result of problems foreseen or self inflicted.

The fact that senior newspaper editors were among those who had to queue for hours to get to the Millennium Dome on New Year's Eve may explain why the Government has had such a bad time.

To be fair, the extent and virulence of the winter flu epidemic is clearly a factor beyond Government's immediate control, though the traditional winter pressure on hospital beds was predicted. Perhaps some Ministers might have wished they had gone down with one of this year's strains just in order to take the pressure off them!

However, perhaps the real test of the integrity of our political system is to gauge the reaction of the political opposition to this series of calamities.

Because walking the tight rope between cheap political opportunism in which the misfortune of others is seized upon with indecent pleasure, and the genuine scrutiny of the wisdom of Government decisions and actions is difficult if you want to be taken seriously. But I'm not sure that that is what many in Parliament want.

After a series of banana skins, scandals and reminders of corruption on their own side (from Archer[6], to Aitken[7], to Hamilton[8] and Ashcroft[9], etc) and the defection of one more of their own number (Shaun Woodward[10]) the Conservatives are not just relieved to have the boot on the other foot, but are making sure that they put the boot in good and proper too.

Indeed, in what I imagine was really a late Christmas present to an opposition politician, Trade Minister Richard Caborn went out of his way to open the whole Government up for full blown criticism. This was during my debate last week on the financial arrangements for Objective One regions (which include Cornwall and Scilly).[11]

After some unscripted and candid answers to straight questions the Minister managed to offend most of the people on the ground who had put the Objective One programmes together. No wonder he wanted to arrange another meeting with me soon to look at the matter again.

FOR SINS obviously committed in some previous life I have found myself placed on a Standing Committee to go through line-by-line scrutiny of the "Child Support, Pensions and Social Security Bill"; commencing last week and scheduled to run all day every Tuesday and Thursday for the next six weeks. I envy those whose job it is to watch paint dry.

It proves how unjust life is. After all, the fiasco of the Child Support Agency was something created by MPs of all parties in previous parliaments. It is they who should be made to put right their own mistakes.

But junior MPs have to accept a fate so lovingly mapped out for us by our senior colleagues.

At least I know how (assuming I get the chance) to treat new MPs after the next General Election!

25th January 2000

[1] *Jack Straw came under fire in January 2000 for allowing suspected Nazi war criminal, Konrad Kalejs, to leave the country after police said there was insufficient evidence to hold him.*
[2] *On 13th January 2000 Jack Straw took the decision not to extradite General Pinochet to Spain under a section of the 1989 extradition act. This requires him not to extradite an alleged offender if it would be "unjust or oppressive" to do so. The decision was reached after controversial medical tests on the ageing former dictator.*
[3] *The boxer, Mike Tyson, was allowed to enter Britain on 16th January 2000, despite immigration rules, which state that entry into Britain should be refused to anyone who has committed a crime that would carry a 12 month jail term; except on compassionate grounds.*
[4] *Several papers reported the first rise in crime figures for 6 years on 18th January 2000.*
[5] *On 20th January 2000 the House of Lords defeated the Home Secretary's Bill,*

which would abolish the right of many defendants to trial by jury.

[6]   Jeffery Archer faced expulsion from the Conservative Party in January 2000 after he was forced to stand down as the Tory Party's candidate for London Mayor. Archer had admitted asking a friend to lie in a libel trial. He was eventually imprisoned in July 2001 for perjury and seeking to pervert the course of justice.

[7]   Former Conservative Cabinet Minister Jonathon Aitken was released from prison in January 2000 after serving seven months of an eighteen month sentence for perjury and perverting the course of justice.

[8]   Another former Conservative Cabinet Minister Neil Hamilton conceded defeat in his first legal battle with Mohamed Al Fayed in this month. The "cash for questions" libel trial verdict labelled him corrupt.

[9]   The then Conservative Party Treasurer—Michael Ashcroft—faced fresh questions about his business dealings. In December 1999 The Times had withdrawn suggestions that Ashcroft has been suspected of involvement in laundering drugs money.

[10]   The former Tory Director of Communications—Shaun Woodward—then MP for Witney, crossed the floor of the Commons in December 1999.

[11]   Objective One funding, House of Commons Debates, 11th January 2000.

Of mice and men

I'M A STRONG supporter of tradition. But even I have to accept there are some quaint traditions which, when witnessed from close quarters, are neither quaint nor worth preserving; often because they have become so abused that they are impossible to defend.

Most of those in this category live on, happily unencumbered by the cut and thrust of the real world, in the Houses of Parliament.

The "all night filibuster" is one such tradition. It sounds harmless enough and a remote and antiquated activity of another world when viewed from the reality of life in West Cornwall.

But to observe grown men at the height of their articulate powers, with all of the resources of the nation's primary democratic institution simply filling time with pointless words, just to fill available time—and to do so all night and then all day—surely brings the whole institution into disrepute.

The occasion: Last Tuesday to Wednesday. The subject: The Disqualifications Bill[1]—an admittedly controversial Bill to permit dual democratic representative membership in Southern and Northern Ireland, but a measure which deserved serious debate rather than juvenile antics.

So, the scene was set. On Tuesday night long after the most bemused insomniac in the public gallery had gone home in the hope of greater entertainments, like watching snail racing or train spotting, a handful of Unionist and Conservative members were just getting into their stride.

"On a night not unlike tonight…" the heroes of futility went on. Those who could cope with witnessing this abuse of parliament competed with each other in striking poses of monumental indifference.

"A bloke came up to me…" droned the next speaker. We were agreed that these talents were being wasted on the House at this hour. They should be ranting from a soap box in a High Street somewhere.

"He said to me, he said…" came one of the best offerings. Those sad souls who were still there actually in the chamber in the small hours had become paralysed by the deadly mix of inevitability and pointlessness.

Only the House Mouse mounted a brief protest. It was a brave and fruitless attempt to break the monotony (latterly the Mouse has had the run of the place in the small hours) but his intervention was ignored.

War, pestilence, can-can dancers, Scud missiles would not have deflected the speakers, who were on automatic pilot—having reached new heights of tedium.

THE SHOCKING and tragic killing of a popular and committed Liberal Democrat activist and the injury of MP Nigel Jones in Cheltenham has brought into sharp focus a previously unrecognised vulnerability faced by those in the public eye who are expected to be accessible to all constituents[2].

My office and staff sadly have already had to take some measures to protect ourselves, but it is simply impossible to give ourselves the protection many might expect us to have.

Constituents have a right to seek help from their MP and by far the vast majority of cases which come to me are genuine problems and concerns which my staff and I attempt to resolve. Of course there are inevitably a tiny minority of vexatious and frivolous cases which come the way of most MPs. The sometimes intemperate attitude of the minority of people who pursue them should not be able to dictate an MP's response to the majority or distance us from the public.

1st February 2000

[1]   See Appendix, page 182.
[2]   *Nigel Jones, Liberal Democrat MP for Cheltenham, was seriously injured and his assistant and long-term friend, Andy Pennington, was killed during an advice surgery for his constituents at his constituency office in the town on 28th January 2000.*

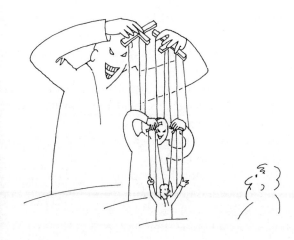

The freak show runs out of control

control freak n. [1960s+] (orig. US) a person who is never satisfied
unless he or she is in absolute control of a situation.) [Cassell's Dictionary of Slang 1998]

IT WAS a bad week for "control freaks". And that's not such a bad thing. Tory leader, William Hague, speaking from the back of his lorry, described Tony Blair as "a control freak who has lost control".

Certainly the attempts by the P.M. to intervene in the devolved Assembly of Wales to save his chosen First Secretary—Alun Michael—should amply demonstrate that human beings tend to take exception if they feel they are being dictated to or manipulated.

Hague was, in fact, closer to the mark than he realised. Certainly Charles Kennedy had been telephoned by Blair to ask him to instruct his party in Wales to back Michael. Three times Blair phoned and three times he was denied.

Charles has this, perhaps old-fashioned, belief that those who are democratically elected should be assumed to be grown up enough to make decisions on their own. So the Assembly in Wales decided without interference from Westminster.

But there is a problem here and I have a lot of sympathy—though no agreement—with the Prime Minister in his predicament.

There is little question that the pressure of high office brings with it expectations of omnipresent leadership and effectiveness which simply cannot be matched by reality. The abnormal lifestyle inevitably creates leaders who become socially and intellectually isolated and whose decisions are better explained by insecurity than by decisiveness.

Last week the PM lost his First Secretary of Wales and this week Blair will have learnt that his favoured candidate for the Mayor of London stands a better chance when he keeps out of it[1].

Fortunately for me, occasional pretentions of self importance and tinpot dictatorship don't seem to last long.

My children, from the age of nought, soon discovered how to wrap me around their little finger and now contain me with terror in case they undermine my credibility with a few well chosen words.

Household pets easily undermine my resolute decisiveness. And my 'free range' guinea pigs regularly outwit me in the garden.

The local MP, a control freak? The very idea would have my parrot falling off his perch with uncontrollable laughter (which is why I don't have one!)

Many of us live in the hope that the massed ranks of control freaks in Westminster might have learnt something during recent weeks, though I doubt it.

Perhaps one day they will realise that the more Herculean their efforts, the more likely they are to generate the very backlash they had wanted to avoid.

I learnt a lesson years ago from the honourable tradition of cussed and obstinate Cornishmen and women down the ages; that the time for control freaks will never come.

15th February 2000

[1]   *On Sunday 20th February 2000 the Prime Minister heard that his favoured candidate for London Mayor won by just 3% over his rival for the Labour Party nomination, Ken Livingstone, in an electoral college that should have worked in Dobson's favour. Livingstone went on to stand and win as an independent candidate. Dobson was beaten into third place after failing to convince Londoners that he had not been foisted upon them by the party leadership. Alun Michael, resigned on Wednesday 9th February 2000, minutes before losing a vote of no confidence in a dramatic instance of political infighting. Mr Michael was widely seen as the Prime Minister's man in Wales, and was replaced, the next day by the man who was widely regarded as the local choice of the Labour Party in Wales, Rhodri Morgan MP AM.*

Clothes? The emperor has no mind either!

I **FOUND** myself having to play the reluctant Party pooper this week.

There is a little-known, small-time gravy train available to lonely and aimless MPs during the long evenings of winter sittings, with free nibbles, sparkling water and occasionally some wine. Every evening there are a series of receptions for good and bad causes.

I had decided to go along to one, to point out what was bad in an otherwise good cause.

It was the well-attended launch of the Campaign for the English Regions in a dining room off the Commons Terrace.

We were going to be told that the Campaign for directly elected Regional Assemblies in Yorkshire, the North East and the North West were well under way and that the campaign for the East Midlands was coming along well too.

The logic was compelling. Wales, Scotland, (to an extent) Northern Ireland and London had secured devolved power so now it was time for the Regions of England.

The vexed questions were about the timetable for this; the powers available to the Regional Assemblies; whether they should have an element of tax raising powers; how they would relate to local government and government regional quangos; how members should be elected and so on. It was all very exciting stuff.

The evangelists for the Regions were astride their high horses galloping forward on the cusp of history in the making.

Amongst all this froth, lather and argument I felt like that boy who pointed out that the Emperor had no clothes. I didn't intend to be churlish but…

"…What do we do if the Region doesn't actually exist?"

The question was met with incomprehension. I was about to engage in a dialogue of the deaf.

To these Regional zealots it was like asking whether we could define the boundaries of God.

IN A SENSE the people of Yorkshire were lucky. The Government Region defined for bureaucratic convenience happened to coincide more-or-less with a region with its own recognisable identity and so it was for the others—to a lesser or greater extent.

But for Cornwall and Scilly, the so-called South West is a Soviet-style construction for people happy to be dragooned into a soulless bureaucracy without a shred of identity and which inspires only career politicians going nowhere and civil servants seeking to be put out to grass.

But they thought that I should be asking how soon a South West campaign could be started.

I tried again.

"The South West doesn't exist, other than as a figment of a diseased imagination or a bureaucrat suffering impersonal boundary-itis. Why destroy a region with a unifying identity (Cornwall) only to create a synthetic region without one?"

I smiled.

Pause. Incomprehension.

They smiled back.

I could see we were going to have problems here. I'll keep you posted.

14th March 2000

Mist of uncertainty gives food for thought

IT HAS BEEN another busy week in Westminster politics. Senior politicians have succeeded, once again, in bringing the honours system into disrepute, by proving—as if proof were still needed—that wealth, greed and special pleading are the qualities most sought after to achieve entry into the modern and exclusive House of Lords[1].

On the one hand politicians never learn and on the other the public understandably find it difficult to distinguish between the good and the downright rotten.

I suppose it's the fact that the dishonourable know that the public take the view that we're "all as bad as each other", which encourages them to carry on regardless. The camouflage of the mist of uncertainty cloaks the guilty with the possibility of innocence and, by association, tars the innocent in the sleaze of guilt.

In a world of uncertainties there is only one thing you can be certain of: protesting your innocence is generally taken as a sign of guilt.

AT THE SAME time politicians are often rightly accused of filling our air waves and column inches with bland sound bites, their own egos and self-importance and generally of interfering too much in our lives; but who otherwise achieve nothing. "What is the point of us?" is a reasonable question to ask.

Well, this week also sees the birth of two new bodies which should have a broadly beneficial impact on our lives. They are the Disability Rights Commission and the Food Standards Agency.

Both are coming into effect with generally all-party support—which is worrying, because the now universally hated Child Support Agency was the last phantom created with this parentage.

The Disability Rights Commission has now come into existence after more than 30 years of quiet revolution in the way that both politicians and the country look upon disability.

The Disability Discrimination Act (1995) was an essential precursor to the Disability Rights Commission Act (1999) and the DRC becomes operational this month. The Commission will work towards eliminating discrimination against disabled people by giving direct advice and assistance, providing a central source of information and advice, carrying out its own research, undertaking formal investigations and offering a conciliation service to help resolve disputes over access, services and facilities[2].

The Food Standards Agency on the other hand has been set up to promote an independent service to generally improve food standards, hygiene and will also have a role in advising on healthy eating[3].

At the Committee Stage of the Food Standards Bill last year I had warned against the possible misuse of the Agency by large food processors and retailers to drive up costs and thus put their small, locally based competitors out of business. We had successfully driven the Government off the proposal of a flat rate registration charge which would have discriminated against smaller operators.

Yet one of the first things the new Agency has done is to introduce a new flat rate charge for butchers irrespective of size. If this trend continues the pressure will be on to undermine the viability of the many smaller and very individual food suppliers and processors—ice cream makers, small abattoirs, local bakers, cheese makers and many other producers. They not only add to the local distinctiveness of our regions, but also to the local economy.

If the Food Standards Agency can achieve just one thing, it should help to support small scale local variety and help small businesses counteract the forces leading towards bland uniformity. The problem with having a few large producers rather than many small ones is that when there is a food poisoning incident it becomes a major incident.

4th April 2000

[1]   Michael Ashcroft was controversially elevated to the House of Lords at the end of March 2000. The former Tory Treasurer had given £1 million to his Party each year since 1997. His nomination had previously been vetoed by the Public Honours Scrutiny Committee, which objected to his residency and citizenship of the Central American tax haven of Belize.
[2]   DRC Helpline, Freepost MID 02164, Stratford-upon-Avon, CV37 9BR.
[3]   Food Standards Helpline, Room 245, Aviation House, 125 Kingsway, London, WC2B 6NH.

The meek are still waiting
...for their inheritance

IT IS EASTER time and news that a political leader will be addressing a gathering of the Evangelical Alliance this weekend will put the fear of God into some[1].

Murmurs in Church aisles and corridors of power will once again echo to the question of whether politics and religion can mix. Politicians have nothing to fear here. But the protectors of the faiths should be wary of a recurring tendency amongst politicians to claim that God is on their side.

Personally, I have always welcomed letters from constituents who are informed by their faith—whether Christian or otherwise. Some others do not.

CERTAINLY it is true that scattered amongst the sack loads of serious weekly mail, those who are slightly mad, eccentric or possessed by demons are found to be magnetically attracted to MPs. "The obsessive, the weird and devotees of strange cults are known to ventilate at length and on a regular basis."[2] Needless to say, none of these are from my constituency, but for some MPs they create a justification to ignore all religiously inspired correspondence as the self evident rantings of the terminally insane.

On the other hand some MPs compete to become the "divine messenger"[3] of the House of Commons. A monastic lifestyle, a churchly voice, loud references to hair shirts and going early to bed alone with a spartan bedtime beverage help to create the right effect.

For the common or garden miserable sinner these sacred messengers seem to glow with the halo of moral superiority, though they are assumed not to be on anyone's boozy party list.

But those politicians who admit to have no greater pretension than to be mere occupants of this world have a right to seek a usable truth.

POLITICIANS seeking the solace of a user-friendly system of values for this world in religious truths can also find themselves faced with as many questions as those seeking political truth.

Is God loving, forgiving and understanding or is He judgemental, intolerant and vengeful? Does "charity *begin* at home?" or does "charity begin at home (and not *end* there)"? Should the meek inherit the earth, or must they pass the Parable of the Talents' qualification?

The God—Whose unassailable approval some politicians believe they can secure—may take the view that there can be 'no certainties in politics as in religion', that Utopia is unobtainable, that there are no absolutes and that we can only strive to improve while being true to ourselves and our consciences.

THE LAST TIME I used the word "conscience" in the House of Commons I was informed by one honourable member that every time he hears a politician using that word he "reaches for (his) sick bag!" And so he might.

But just as all people, especially the religious, should listen to politicians with a healthy dose of scepticism, so should politicians be allowed to question the motives of others.

Politics may be the art of discovering your view/position/prejudice first and then seeking the evidence to support it afterwards.

Similarly, it hasn't escaped the notice of politicians that some faiths have zealots amongst their ranks who appear to seek to use it as a respectable front from which to pursue political and moral vendettas against other people whose views, lifestyles, up-bringing, inclinations and even cultural and racial origins are not to their approval.

Some of the parallels can be very disturbing, but, at heart, politics and religion can mix. They generate a volatile and creative cocktail, but, in a climate of tolerance and mutual respect, I believe that some good can emerge.

The inspired, Christian-based Jubilee 2000 campaign to write off third world debt is a shining example.

The meek are still patiently awaiting their rightful inheritance. Politicians keep promising it will arrive tomorrow (or the day after). But religions know that politicians will become complacent if they are not constantly challenged to bring that day closer.

18th April 2000

[1]   *Many papers reported on a substantial gathering of people at holiday camps in Skegness in Lincolnshire and Minehead in Somerset under the Evangelical Alliance during April 2000. William Hague addressed the Minehead camp.*
[2]   *Paul Flynn MP in "Commons Knowledge" (p.63)*
[3]   *Paul Flynn MP in "Commons Knowledge" (p.29)*

Don't let the Apathy Party win again

MPS RETURNING to Westminster after the Easter week recess would be wise to mask any healthy tan obtained on a foreign holiday; unless they can prove—with war wounds and battle scars—that it was a by-product of hard graft on the door step in the Romsey by-election, local elections or the London mayoral smog.

I recently spent a day in Romsey—testing temperature, joining the candidate at a public meeting and applauded by activists for apparently miraculously finding my way to the HQ by two trains, a bus and on foot and without demanding a V.I.P chauffeur driven limousine for the last 20 or so miles.

Of course, like all politicians, I most feared, not supporters of other parties, but voters who issued a plague on all politicians.

Things had been going quite well for me, but towards the end of an afternoon canvas in a leafy suburb of Romsey I was greeted on the doorstep by a middle-aged woman with:

"I don't know. I'm just losing faith in all politicians."

To which I replied:

"Please don't say that, because I might start to lose faith in the electorate."

We laughed at this contradiction and chatted about some of the things that had turned her off—the effect of successive governments' treatment of pensioners in particular.

We parted on good terms. Whether she would ultimately vote in

Candidate George with son Davy and daughter Morvah at Ruan Minor, General Election Day, 1992

this election I have no idea, but our exchange was typical of many—based on a belief that politicians are a species all of their own—not real human beings but cold blooded, thick skinned reptilian beings transplanted from a nether world, yet given super human powers to turn the vaguest wish immediately into automatic reality.

The worry is that some politicians, I think, have started to believe this about themselves.

Of course, the truth is that many MPs are probably more sensitive than most realise—not to gratuitous abuse, but to a reminder of their own fallibility.

We haven't (and shouldn't have) ready answers for everything, and the electorate should be deeply weary of any politician who hasn't got the phrases "I don't know", "I am sorry", "I got it all wrong" or "I hadn't thought of that" amongst their vocabulary.

Electors shouldn't lose faith in all politicians nor in the political process. Disillusionment is what some politicians want; it gives them the power to take the electorate for granted. Tin pot dictators emerge from a massive turn out of apathy.

Whether it be a Parliamentary by-election, a London mayoral bash or the Penwith local elections I urge you to continue using your votes.[1]

2nd May 2000

[1]   *On 4th May 2000, Sandra Gidley (Liberal Democrat) won the Romsey by-election, Ken Livingstone MP (Independent) the London Mayoral election and the Penwith local elections finished with a continuation of a council with no overall political control*

103

Imprisoned with Blair babes & Baby

WHEN PEOPLE complain that politicians are out of touch with the real world they should be offering us their sympathy, not their contempt.

News came this week that one of the 1997 intake of young MPs —and a recent mother of twins—has decided to quit parliament at the next general election, because of the long and anti-social working hours and the juvenile public school attitude of many of the old guard.[1]

The juvenile public school boys have seen this as a cause for celebration rather than contrition, and just for good measure kept the house up last (Monday) night until 2.30 am because they thought it would be a good wheeze prolonging a debate on how long we should debate the Royal Parks Trading Bill (a bill which primarily deals with the crucial questions of the siting of mobile burger bars in some of London's parks).

One will have a double cheesy egg mega burger, hold the onions

FRED'S BURGERS

I don't think MPs can complain about the pressure and the long hours. After all, it is a job which many others regularly and very publicly compete to take from you. But I do think that we can and should complain about the repeated and obscene misuse of public and parliamentary time and resources.

EARLIER in the evening I had briefly spoken on an uncontentious piece of minor legislation on grants to the fishing industry.

The bill should have been nodded through and certainly both Liberal Democrat and Tory opposition front benchers had no quarrel with it. But a handful of Tory pranksters decided that it would be a wow to detain the house for awhile by forcing a division (a vote) and so we did. Result: Ayes (i.e. in favour) 313; Noes (i.e. against) 1.[2] Oh how they must have chortled. What a wheeze! What fun!

And how angry you must be, dear reader, to hear that tax payers' money is being spent and that our democratic system is being abused by this puerile nonsense.

Some have described Parliament as the most luxurious prison in the country. As I claim not to have seen any of the others I'm not in a position to assess, but a kind of prison it is, if not an asylum.

MPs from the South East who have homes to go to at night want the hours of the place reformed so that they can be with their families and constituents in the evening—meaning shorter days but longer weeks. But MPs from the Celtic fringes (Cornwall, Scotland, Wales and Northern Ireland) want the days reformed so that they can have quality time in their constituencies for long weekends—meaning longer days and shorter parliamentary weeks.

REFORMING parliament so that MPs had free evenings in London would be bad news for London's night life and seriously worrying for Party whips. MPs with long free evenings could get up to lots of mischief up in town. It would be like letting animals out of a zoo.

The Prime Minister—a "modern man" of sorts—can, of course, and should take time off to be with his family now that the new baby has arrived[3] but by the time he comes back we should have resolved how to deal with the parliamentary pranksters so that we can all get a good night's sleep at the end of a long and seriously hard working day.

23rd May 2000

[1]   *Tess Kingham, then MP for Gloucester.*
[2]   *Sea Fishing Grants (Charges) Bill, House of Commons Debates, 22nd May 2000, column 755.*
[3]   *Leo Blair was born on the 20th May 2000. The PM took two weeks' paternity leave.*

A region that offers antiseptic oblivion

NEWS THAT "senior figures…are being approached to lead a new campaign to establish regional government in the South West" (*WMN 27th May 2000*) was an appropriately light story for a Bank Holiday weekend.

However, my concern is that the now routine resounding disinterest and apathy with which the general populace of this non-existent region respond may only serve to encourage the minor empire builders and anoraks behind this mindless nonsense.

Most normal folk demonstrate a level of enthusiasm and patriotism for the "South West Region" (sic) which extends to being able hardly to stifle a yawn at the mere hint of the subject being mentioned.

True, the Government failed to honour its pre-election promise of setting up a Cornish Development Agency, to set up instead a seven counties Development Agency for the South West; but this is primarily a functional institution: either it succeeds in helping local economic development projects with professional support and money or fails by masquerading as a "strategic" entity which attempts to generate a synthetic regional identity. Whether it be based in Exeter, Bristol or Birmingham for that matter is largely immaterial.

True again, a Regional Chamber has been established, but this is merely a talking shop; a pleasant and agreeable talking shop with pleasant and agreeable people, but a talking shop nonetheless.

That some are getting so carried away with this that they genuinely believe public torpor can be interpreted as enthusiasm to set up directly elected regional bodies with real decision-making powers has, I concede, proved how wrong I was.

I admit to being a member of the "if we ignore them they'll probably go away" brigade but I hadn't properly accounted for the speed at which the vacuum left by disinterest is filled by nonsense unless, in the meantime, common sense prevails. Many had thought the idea of setting up regional government for an invented South West of England so laughable and absurd as not to be worth honouring with the effort of the intellectual drubbing it deserves. This is probably still the case but perhaps now a clearer demolition of these proposals needs to be completed before they gain any crumbs of serious currency.

THOSE OF US WHO are concerned about the gathering apathy and low turn outs at election time have a double reason not to give the creation of standardised regions a single crumb of comfort or encouragement. The pathetically low turn out at the last local elections would surely be eclipsed by reaching new heights of lethargy in an unimpressed electorate faced with a bland, uniform and characterless region.

If we were to decentralise some powers from an over-centralised state we should do so to places and regions which actually exist, to territories about which people actually give a damn.

For Cornwall, the only region is Cornwall (and Scilly, if it were to chose to come on board, but have its own distinctiveness respected). But such ideas face such established misunderstandings it's difficult to take so called "conventional wisdom" much beyond a mindless "base camp".

The first criticism is always that of dismissiveness or to diminish the concept; i.e. "don't be silly"; "you can't be serious". But if you look at the alternatives it is the only serious option available.

Secondly, we'll be told that such a notion would be inconvenient; i.e. "it's too late"; "it would cause too many problems"; "where would it leave everybody else?" But this fails to recognise that decentralisation can be untidy. A settlement, which reflects community, identity and idiosyncrasy, doesn't fall neatly into uniform bureaucratic patterns.

The third criticism is that Cornwall is too small. It has a population of about half a million when the standardised regions are supposed to be ten times that size. But our problem is that we have become too insular in our outlook. If we lift our sights above the narrow horizons of the UK we only need to look at regions both in Europe and elsewhere to see that regions and provinces vary in size.

A recent brief visit to Canada demonstrated this to me. Provinces like Prince Edward Island (138,000), Newfoundland (541,000), New Brunswick (755,000) and Nova Scotia (939,000)—all have the same powers as Quebec (7.3 million) and Ontario (11.5 million). Where service delivery (such as specialist medical services) requires economies of scale or a large critical mass then they have no difficulty in overcoming this by co-operation between provinces.

Even criticisms that a Cornish region would be too insular doesn't stand up to analysis. Any such initiative would open up opportunities for Cornwall in a much wider world. Instead of cutting itself off it would enable Cornwall to cut itself into the celebration of diversity of communities, cultures, languages and tradition here in the UK and elsewhere.

The primary down side would be that such an initiative would give succour to a handful of certifiable nationalists—but they are so few in number that there would be no tolerance for this. The prospect of compulsory kilt wearing and constant reference to genealogy would soon become tiresome.

Cornwall has a choice—it can pick itself up from its torpor in the face of a deeply anaesthetised region and it can stand up for itself, or it can simply allow itself to sleep walk into an antiseptic oblivion.

Written for the Western Morning News
30th May 2000

Reaping what we sow

THERE ARE times when I can feel nothing other than shame to be in and therefore associated with what happens in Parliament. It is my adult equivalent of feeling myself go bright crimson when a teacher demands of a whole class at school that a miscreant own up for his crime—despite (occasionally!) being blameless. It was probably a result of all those "miserable sinner" sermons on Sunday mornings at Chapel in Mullion.

But to receive reports of the exceptional thuggery and hooliganism of the English in Europe[1] and the indescribable tragedy of the 58 Chinese refugees dying in such appalling circumstances on a container lorry to Britain[2], it is only right that all politicians in Westminster consider where we got it wrong and how we can put it right.

I DID SEE the golden opportunity of a question to the Prime Minister a week before, to launch an attack on those politicians who stoke up racial intolerance by "artfully blaming asylum seekers, blaming Europe and blaming foreigners at every opportunity" and warn that we would "reap what we sow".[3]

We witnessed some of this on the beach near Long Rock where it is alleged that a visiting party of young people from Germany were attacked. The good people who live at Long Rock and Marazion were as shocked and appalled as the rest of us.

The problem is that we as politicians are now "reaping what we sow".

The Commons debate on the discovery of the dead at Dover heard a lot of "condolences" and shock but little in the way of responsibility.

I have before pointed out in this column the inconsistency in the 1951 Geneva Convention which calls on signatories to offer sanctuary to refugees who claim to have a "well founded fear of persecution" but has nothing to say on how those refugees are to get into these countries in the first place—unless of course they get here illegally. This is especially the case with Britain.

The present system gives encouragement to illegal refugee traffickers, because they know that genuine asylum seekers must break the law before getting protection.

SO WHAT message have we sent out to the wider world this week—a week in which our best known ambassadors abroad have excelled themselves in the streets and bars of Belgium and our welcoming hospitality has seen appalling and tragic death on a mass scale?

The nature of debate in the Commons sets the tone of these events.

If we reap what we sow then it's time we got rid of the seeds of invasive knotweed—the seeds sown by bigoted bar room bores and tabloid editors—and showed leadership by sowing seeds of intelligent enquiry and tolerance, irrespective of how unfashionable these qualities appear to be these days.

20th June 2000

[1]   *England's victory against Germany in the European Cup—their first for 34 years —was overshadowed by the arrest of over 500 hooligans in Belgium.*
[2]   *58 Chinese immigrants suffocated in the back of a sealed truck attempting to enter Britain through Dover on 18th June 2000.*
[3]   *See Appendix, page 182.*

Know thine enemy

THE GREAT THING about having "enemies" is that you know them. You can recognise them. When you see them they have little red horns and forked tails and their eyeballs bulge when they speak to you. Generally, we politicians like to have known "enemies" because it helps us define our own boundaries. In fact, it is probably true for us all that we tend to get more passionate about the things we disagree with than those things with which we agree.

So political "enemies" are a necessary and welcome part of political life. Imagine then, having "enemies" within your own ranks. Sometimes you know who they are but often you don't.

STORIES of politicians and spin-doctors "briefing" against each other have been rife in Westminster during recent weeks.[1]

Whether it is true or not is for others to judge. The fact is that any politician who becomes so anxious that they wish to "manage" news and events, usually ends up managed by it themselves.

The biggest problem, however, is being aware of the enemy within. Providing it is from a respectable distance, it is fascinating to watch the process of self destruction and it is remarkable to watch this process happening to a Government which has been dealt such a strong hand—a thumping parliamentary majority, a strong economy and optimistic public expenditure estimates.

But when the process of self destruction spills over into being accident prone you know you've got serious problems.

No doubt we can all imagine ourselves applauding the Prime Minister as he promised us that local thugs and hooligans would be humbled as they were frog-marched by Dixon-of-Dock-Greens down to the closest cash machine to pay up for their anti-social behaviour.[2]

But imagining that this might happen without further incident, that criminals masquerading as The Bill wouldn't take advantage of the mildly inebriated and extract money from them and that a whole load of other practical problems could be overcome, would be naïve.

GIVEN the Prime Minister's luck there was an inevitability about his family's own highly publicised drunken brush with the law only days later.[3] To be fair, most people can sympathise with the P.M. at this time.

Parliament is at a fascinating stage. Most realists accept that political parties don't so much "win" elections as their opponents "lose" them. Judging by current form, the wisest advice for opposition parties at present is to sit back, do nothing and wait for power to drop into your laps!

4th July 2000

[1] *During June and July 2000 various feuds were reported amongst senior Government Ministers. On the 19th June The Telegraph reported how Tony Blair sought to prevent arguments within the Cabinet over the euro by forcing Gordon Brown and Robin Cook into a display of unity by sharing an aircraft with him to attend an EU summit in Portugal. The move followed "renewed feuding" over Mr Brown's attempts to make himself the guardian of the conditions for determining whether Britain should join the single currency after the forthcoming election. John Prescott, the Deputy Prime Minister, pitched into the row with a blunt reminder to Mr Brown— who on Friday spoke of how "this Treasury" would decide if the conditions were met— that the Cabinet would make the final decision.*
[2] *In a leaked memo, it emerged that the Prime Minister had suggested on the spot fines for drunken behaviour.*
[3] *The Prime Minister's son, Euan Blair, aged 16, was reprimanded by police for being "drunk and incapable" after celebrating the end of his GCSEs on Friday 7th July 2001 in London's Leicester Square.*

A holiday in the chair

SPARE A THOUGHT for the poor MPs who have just the period between now and the middle of October to catch up on all those constituency matters, visits, reports to their constituents, preparations for the packed parliamentary session ahead, and fine-tuning their memoirs.[1]

Of course, some actually find time for a holiday!

As many of them will, at one point or another, be coming to this constituency, I'll find myself in the position of a sitting duck for those who will be canvassing for support in their campaign to become the next Commons Speaker.[2]

The difficulty they all face is that all MPs are away from Westminster until 23rd October when the first item of business will be the election of the new Speaker. The opportunities to get into huddles or to whip up a healthy conspiracy against your opponent has been limited and it is just possible, that instead of the conventional "stitch-up" behind the scenes, the election will actually be based on the merit of those MPs putting themselves forward. Most people suspect it to be a "control freak's" nightmare.

The alternative would be the prospect of witnessing frantic candidates trampling over the most exclusive beaches of the world to disturb the most unhealthy looking bodies to plead for their support.

AFTER last week's promised spending spree by the Chancellor, Gordon Brown, most MPs are pouring over the small print of the Comprehensive Spending Review to find out where the catch is.[3]

Although the announcements are welcome and news that public

finances are healthy is unquestionably good news, the event itself is a little like receiving one of those unsolicited envelopes in the post which tell you that you're the lucky winner of a prize and to please open it to find out more.

For us, there is important news that the Government claims that it will—after a lot of campaigning—guarantee to match European money under Cornwall's Objective One programme. This should be a cause for celebration, except that evidence that the Government has the means of delivering this money efficiently to projects on the ground has yet to be demonstrated.

With this in mind, my Cornish Parliamentary colleagues, Paul Tyler, Colin Breed and I spent a day this week talking to the Irish Government to find out how they made such a storming success of Objective One in their country during the 90s.[4]

What came across at every level was an attitude of mind which simply wasn't prepared to contemplate failure.

It wasn't so much a "can do" attitude—they were more confident than that—it was a "see no reason why we can't" approach.

The Irish don't need the luck of the Irish, they just make things happen.

25th July 2000

[1]   *Parliament rose on 28th July 2000 and resumed on 23rd October 2000.*
[2]   *The former speaker of the House, the Rt. Hon. Betty Boothroyd announced her retirement on 12th July 2000, the announcement took MPs unaware and led to an unprecedented burst of applause from all sides of the House.*
[3]   *The Comprehensive Spending Review was released by the Chancellor on the 18th July 2000. The biggest news was the rise in the NHS budget from £44,485m in 2000 to £56,653m in 2003/4, a 27.3% cash increase over three years. The personal social services budget also rose from £9,407m to £12,208m over the same period, a cash increase of 29.7%.*
[4]   *MPs visit to Dublin, 23rd-24th July 2000.*

Fuelling the debate

THERE **IS** always a problem for those politicians who escape to out of the way places during the parliamentary recess. Because, while the cat's away the mice of political fiction can come out to play.

For example, one national matter which rightly concerns many here in West Cornwall and in Scilly is that of the almost crippling fuel costs which are currently imposed on business and domestic users.

However, amongst all the "spin" and finger pointing what is perhaps most fascinating about the current debate is the opportunity for cross party agreement on how to resolve the problems of high fuel duty.

Because, although it is true that my Liberal Democrat colleagues in the House of Commons and I led the debate against recent proposed increases in fuel duty and criticised both the Conservatives who introduced the "fuel duty escalator" and the Labour Government who kept the escalator going for longer than they should have done, the fact is that all parties recognise that there is a problem both of congestion, pollution and use of non-renewable fuel which needs to be resolved.

So amid all the claim and counter-claim the question should not be about who did what first and who can successfully prove that the other is at fault, but how a sensible balance is to be struck.[1]

THE FACT is that there are 22 million registered cars in the UK today, when there were only 2 million in 1950. 70 per cent of the population have access to at least one car whereas only 14 percent had this in 1950. It is estimated that 380 billion vehicle-kilometres are travelled each year in the UK when the figure was only 26 billion in 1950.

Against this, half of all car journeys in London are less than two miles and one fifth of the time in a car in London is spent stationary! The average speed in London is 11 miles per hour—the same as a Victorian horse and carriage—some progress!

In fact, it has been estimated by the RAC that 45 per cent of car journeys are "unnecessary" and could be easily made by public transport. Perhaps the most worrying factor is that vehicle numbers, distances travelled and congestion are all predicted to rise steeply, despite the high cost of private travel.

Presently road congestion and pollution from it cost businesses £20 billion per annum (according to the CBI); cost motorists £23 billion (according to the RAC); cause 3 thousand deaths and bring forward 24 thousand deaths per annum (according the British Medical Association); cause millions of people to live above the World Health Organisation (WHO) safe noise level limits, aggravate asthma for millions of people and significantly contribute to global warming (transport is the fastest growing source of CO_2).

CLEARLY, SIMPLY allowing private car usage to mushroom and taking the view that demand for increase in use should simply be accommodated would be politically irresponsible and would certainly compromise future generations.

The fundamental challenge is that we establish a policy which is able to make a distinction between those arguably "unnecessary" journeys in the congested centres and the "necessity" for private car ownership in those parts of the country, like ours.

This is the opportunity for us all to chip into the debate because certainly our party—like, I imagine, the other main parties—are undertaking a fundamental review of policy in this area—and if the others aren't they certainly should be.

I am arguing that we should freeze the level of fuel duty for a five year period—at least not increase duty over the level of inflation—

and to promote further a long held Liberal Democrat policy of using the "stick" and "carrot" of taxation and tax breaks to encourage fuel efficiency, liquid petroleum gas use and business rate reduction measures to support small independent petrol retailers.

Against this the emphasis of policy should be upon discouraging unnecessary journeys in city centres and on congested routes that coincide with the provision of adequate public transport, and ensuring that rural residents in places like West Cornwall, rural Scotland and Wales—where private car ownership is a necessity—are not unfairly penalised.

Inviting drivers to collectively "dump the pump" on certain days[2] is a nonsense and will have zero effect on government policy—whereas a well argued policy proposal which can be picked up and made to work would have an infinitely greater chance of success.

8th August 2000

[1]   *Fuel blockades lasted from 7th until 14th September 2000.*
[2]   *1st August 2000 was designated "dump the pump" day, to allow motorists to show anger at high petrol prices by boycotting petrol stations.*

"Away the lads"

WHEN ALL else fails, lower your standards", read the T-shirt slogan noticed recently.

It could have been a motto for politicians who more often than not find there are fewer votes in 'high principle' than in populist 'low politics'.

But, perhaps it also represents a motto for an increasingly beleaguered minority: that 49% of the population of this country who will discover today[1] that the GCSE results will show a record gender gap with girls outperforming boys. This now suggests an unbreachable rift in ability between the 'fair' and the (presumably) 'unfair' sexes.

As if to anticipate this coffin nail, one political leader, in what will become for him an indelible remark, assumed that bravado about conventionally pub-crawling his way through 14 pints of Best during his younger working day would win admirers amongst the protectors of empty headed 'Laddish' culture.[2]

Apart from being improbable and absurd, that claim proved two things we now know to be true. The first is that politicians have a terminal inability to resist telling porky scratchings and the second, perhaps more devastating, is the common perception that men can only impress other men if they descend to the lowest available standards.

For me, one of the problems I have in representing the very constituency in which I was born and brought up is that there is no chance of embellishing the past in an attempt to make my life's experience seem more remarkable or glamorous than it was.

It is fortunate that at times like this I can rest happy in the certain knowledge that my youth was the exceptionally forgettable boredom of a hapless nonentity. Any suggestion that it was anything else would invite the certainty of a humiliating public contradiction.

22nd August 2000

1] Written on 22nd for publication on 24th August (date of publication of GCSE results).

2] Revealed this week for an interview in men's magazine GQ, William Hague claimed that, as a teenager, he often drank "14 pints of best a day".

Old lessons from Newfoundland

REPORT OF TWO brief conversations I had at Newlyn Fish Festival.[1]
I believe they tell a story.

1. Leading Councillor of Cornwall County Council
(*Cornwall: population 500,000*) approaching me with a question:

"What's all this about you and the other MPs signing a declaration for a Cornish Assembly? Are you serious? What powers do you think this Assembly will have?"

I replied: "Modest additional powers agreed between ourselves and Central Government. Anyway, isn't the County Council now just a souped-up Parish Council? All your powers have been taken away from you. What actual decision making powers has the County Council got?"

Leading Councillor : "Well I'll have to get back to you on that one. I can't answer questions like that off the top of my head."

2. Brian Tobin—Premier of Newfoundland, Canada
(*Newfoundland: population about 550,000*).

"Provincial Government in Canada is well established and is a foundation of the social and political life of which we are justly proud. There are few things we can't do for ourselves at provincial level and the Canadian National Government has to consult us closely before passing any legislation that might affect our Province."

I replied: "But what do you say to people who claim that your Province is too small?"

Brian Tobin: "Just look at our record. And in any case, look at a country like Iceland with half the people of Newfoundland. They are one of the wealthiest and most successful countries on earth!"

As most people who met him acknowledge, Brian Tobin is a bright articulate and charismatic politician and one who I would tip as a future Prime Minister of Canada.

Although the contrast in attitude could hardly be more stark, I do hope that we genuinely learn lessons from "our old friends" from across the Atlantic.

Not only should we learn from the decimation of cod stocks before it' too late here, but we might also learn a great deal from the form and style of their Provincial Government.

29th August 2000

[1]   The festival was held on the 28th August 2000 and was officially opened by former Canadian Fisheries Minister and Premier of Newfoundland and Labrador, Brian Tobin MP.

Andrew and Brian Tobin, Premier of Newfoundland, at Newlyn Fish Festival

Fuelling the bandwagon

SOME ASPECTS of politics are predictable. In fact, it is an unspoken fact of political life that if, when bad news strikes unexpectedly and you are caught without your political briefings in place and you have nothing intelligent to say, then you should knit your brow, strike up a purposeful pose, drop your voice about half an octave and demand a ministerial resignation. After all, it takes little imagination and sounds terribly decisive!

Of course, I am no fan of the Millennium Dome and never have been and would be happy to take my place as a fully paid-up vice president of the "I told you so" brigade where the Dome is concerned.

I am sure that on the day it emerged that yet another £47million of lottery money was being thrown at the Dome to help bail it out until the end of the year, Culture Minister Lord Falconer,[1] would not have been "blown over with a feather duster" at the news that there was a chorus of opposition politicians (including some from my Party), newspaper editors and others who were calling for his resignation. I suppose that the problem for the Government is that if ministerial heads were to roll every time there was a whiff of bad news from or about the Millennium Dome, there would be no-one left in Parliament, let alone a Government to carry the can.

But to hear leading politicians who shared in collective Cabinet responsibility when the fateful decision was made to support this dubious adventure must take one of the many biscuits that should be given during this extended silly season in which every bandwagon going has been jumped on for all its worth.

What will stick in the craw of those of us in West Cornwall and on the Isles of Scilly who shared my original scepticism about the Millennium Dome is that the ease with which national leaders can be seduced into spending multi-millions of pounds of public money on a grandiose black hole is in inverse proportion to the immense difficulty we will find in clawing the relative small change we require to get more modest but significant investments started under the Objective One programme in what is one of the poorest, if not *the* poorest region in the UK.

WITNESSING the queues at every petrol station as supplies dried up had me guessing what it would be like if there were a politician rather than an oil shortage. Would there be a public panic with queues forming in case the supply of politicians ran out?

Just imagine it. There'd be no easy target for people's frustrations, anxieties and derision. Television companies would eventually have no-one to call on to put a veneer of falsehood over a tissue of lies! And comedians would struggle to entertain us as their prime source of comic material dried up.

But just as we will find that a world with far fewer cars is a much more pleasant one I know that if we were presented with a world with fewer politicians, the public would never have us back!

12th September 2000

[1] *Millennium Commission members agreed to give the Millennium Dome an extra £47m of National Lottery money on 5th September 2000. The money was said to be a "maximum" amount. The decision follows repeated assurances from Dome organisers that it would not seek any more funds from the Commission. In making the extra money available, the Commission said it was "deeply disappointed" to be in a position to have to offer a further grant.*

Acute questioning

IT STILL staggers me that when a politician trips over or makes any kind of mistake it is "big news". I would have thought that the electorate is well used to the idea of politicians not being infallible.

However, the more infallible politicians imply that they are the more pleasure we get from pointing out their fallibilities.

So it was that this week, after watching the Shadow Home Secretary fall down a manhole of her own digging,[1] the impression will be given that most leading politicians are poorly reformed 'dope heads' who enjoy tub-thumping about law and order.

IN FACT, very little in politics is really about attempts to knock chunks out of each other, as many important decisions in which politicians have to engage are in fact not in any way party political. This week the whole community here in West Cornwall has an opportunity to commence a public debate on what is probably the most important public service provided in the area—namely West Cornwall Hospital.[2]

As someone who is encouraging a more open public debate about the future of the hospital, I would always have to commence any comment with an acknowledgement. I hold those who have been so deeply involved in considering the hospital's future in the highest regard and certainly appreciate that their intentions are honourable. That does not mean to say that we should accept without question the results of the process in which they have been engaged.

The first problem for members of the public who are anxious about the future of the hospital is to untangle what is actually being proposed. A report I have received from the local Primary Care

Group—which has co-ordinated the discussions—concludes that "emergency services at West Cornwall Hospital do have to change"—but that phrase could have been taken from a political dictionary of "weasel words" as it doesn't indicate whether it should "change" for the better or worse; whether emergency admissions should be bolstered, increased, given more support, reduced or diverted. And this is the nub of the problem.

LAST WEEK'S *Cornishman* editorial put its finger on the nub of the subject when it said that what we want to know is "what needs to be done to maintain existing services at the hospital?"

So far there's been no "input/output" analysis—in other words, no comparing how many patients come in to West Cornwall, what clinical procedures are performed and what the result is and how that compares with Treliske.

We need to understand why the consultant cardiologist's post at West Cornwall Hospital was not re-advertised and why the echo-cardiogram has been removed in recent months.

The Royal Colleges (of Physicians and Surgeons) may well advise that the resources and specialists available at West Cornwall are no longer appropriate in this day and age to maintain the current services and that the doctors' training posts, which are essential to the running of the hospital, are no longer sustainable. But to decide that this means that West Cornwall should significantly reduce its emergency admissions is not a decision pre-ordained by God. It is one which everyone of us has the right to challenge and to demand that alternatives are looked at.

Alternatives should involve exploring how many of the Government's proposed additional 7,500 consultants, 20,000 new nurses and over 6,500 therapists could come and work at the Royal Cornwall Hospitals Trust and have a role at West Cornwall. We should also ask how many of the 7,000 extra hospital beds the Government proposes to create should come to West Cornwall and in a scenario where the Government plans to build over 100 new hospitals by 2010 we should ask whether it is appropriate to reduce emergency admissions at West Cornwall?

Before any decisions are taken we need to investigate what opportunities there are for the development of additional diagnostic facilities and other resources at West Cornwall, especially in circumstances where the Government is proposing to purchase an extra 250 CT scanners.

The bottom line for us all is that for too long West Cornwall has been pliant and grateful. We have accepted what we are told we will get; often without any quarrel at all.

The proposals for West Cornwall are significant. They should be subject to the utmost scrutiny and the alternatives rigorously explored.

As a community we should not accept change at the hospital until: (i) all plausible options have been properly considered; (ii) it is clear that patients' interests are best secured by change; and, (iii) above all, we know that if emergency admissions are diverted to Treliske it will result in a better service. Many people are unconvinced that Treliske could cope and a scenario in future years where many emergency admissions are on "divert to Derriford" is certainly not inconceivable.

This is not a party political issue. It is a very significant one for the community here in West Cornwall and it is one on which every concerned resident has the right to be heard.

10th October 2000

[1] *On 9th October 2000 Ann Widdecombe, then Conservative Shadow Home Secretary, was forced to backtrack on her conference speech pledge of zero tolerance against cannabis users after seven Shadow Cabinet Members effectively mocked the policy by admitting they had used the drug in the past.*
[2] *A Public Meeting was held on 10th October 2000 at the Queens Hotel, Penzance to discuss the future of West Cornwall Hospital*

Speaking out of turn

AS MPS frantically complete their efforts to tie-up all loose ends on their ongoing constituency work during a busy parliamentary recess, they are presented with two reminders of the difficulty facing them in the last parliamentary session before an anticipated general election next May.

The first is the now absurd obsession the national media have for the deeply uninteresting blow by blow account of what Geoffrey Robinson and Peter Mandelson said or didn't say to each other at a private dinner long enough ago for any normal human being to have forgotten the crucial detail.[1]

You'd think by listening to the national media that in constituencies like this, local people "talk of little else" when confronted by their local MP. Nothing can be further from the truth.

With so many serious issues facing the country, it is astounding that an obsession with the private affairs of others takes precedence over the serious crisis facing the small family farmers, the poverty facing many pensioners and the critical negotiations now going on in the Middle East.[2]

The second is the now almost certain prospect that the so-called "Mother of Parliaments" will demonstrate its capacity to be the "Grandfather of the arcane" when it comes to electing its new speaker on our first day back in Parliament this Monday.[3]

Although there are now frantic attempts to pre-empt what will be an absurd process, it is possible that the best paid MP of the lot—higher paid than the Prime Minister—and with vitally important responsibilities to protect Parliament, will be appointed under the democratic equivalent of "Russian roulette".

There could be up to twelve candidates for the job. There is no requirement for them to produce a manifesto, canvassing is not encouraged and one of the most popular candidates may not even have their name put forward. It all depends on the "Father of the House", Sir Edward Heath!

17th October 2000

[1]   The "loan scandal" that forced Peter Mandelson to resign as Trade and Industry
Secretary two years before, came back to haunt him. Mr Mandelson had said to the
Commons Standards and Privileges Committee on 18th May 1999 that "I did not go
to him [Robinson] with the intention of asking him to loan me some money."
Mr Robinson said Mr Mandelson solicited the loan, rather than simply accepted it.
It was argued that this version of events was at odds with Mr Mandelson's statement to
the Commons committee.

[2]   A crisis summit was held at Sharm el-Sheikh, on the Red Sea. Israel and the
Palestinians agreed to an uncertain cease-fire on the 17th October 2000 after pressure
from the US President Bill Clinton.

[3]   The voting for the new speaker, carried out on the evening of Monday 23rd
October was as follows: Sir Alan Haselhurst (Con) lost by 140 to 345; Alan Beith (Lib
Dem) 83 to 409; Gwyneth Dunwoody (Lab) 170 to 341; Sir George Young (Con) 241
to 317; Menzies Campbell (Lib Dem) 98 to 381; David Clark (Lab) 192 to 257;
Nicholas Winterton (Con) 116 to 340; John McWilliam (Lab) 30 to 309; Michael
Lord (Con) 146 to 290; Sir Patrick Cormack (Con) 130 to 287; Richard Shepherd
(Con) 136 to 282.   Final vote: Michael Martin backed by 370 votes to eight.
Michael Martin: victor.

The nah-nee-na-nee-na-nah tendency takes over

AS PARLIAMENT STUMBLES closer to the next general election, it's beginning to look less like a debating chamber and more like a school playground.

Politics is full of tendencies—the "Militant tendency", the "Bolshevik tendency", the "Far Right tendency" and so on—but now an old "tendency" is regaining the upper hand.

It is the "Nah-nee-na-nee-na-nah Tendency". Members of this growing band probably have private gatherings where they can indulge in thumb to ear hand signs and "did"—"didn't"—"did"—"didn't" arguments until they all go off and take their footballs home with them.

In public members of the tendency are required to accuse others of things which other reasonable people might suggest they themselves were guilty of and to constantly seek to outbid each other—"we would give more to pensioners than you would, neah!" "Oh no you wouldn't." You know the sort of stuff.

A cause célèbre of the Nah-nee-na-nee-na-nah Tendency this week has been the blessed Millennium Dome.

An Audit Commission Report has just come out[1] which ends up offering some not unexpected criticisms of how the whole project was handled.

For the Conservatives, who first took the decision to build it, the whole thing is obviously the fault of the Labour Government and Labour Ministers cannot help but point out the crucial involvement of the Tories.

In this game of "pass the exploding parcel" it was poor Lord Falconer who was caught "in possession" of the project when the music stopped.

Yet on any objective assessment it was a catalogue of errors and poor scrutiny the whole way along. Sneering and finger pointing only contributes to the certain sense that this project was destined to fail, however favourable the circumstances were or were not. For my own part I had always opposed the project on the basis that it was impossible to justify spending so much "public" money on a wealthy region when we were being offered such poor crumbs of comfort.

IN CONTRAST, the Chancellor's recent performance at the despatch box[2] extracted maximum satisfaction when he brought out a massive artillery to shoot every Conservative fox in sight, leaving them with just a pea shooter of minor whinges. This demonstrated the importance of not seeking to outbid your opponents without leaving some ammunition in reserve.

On fuel, pensions, company law and most other areas the Conservatives had been undone in the Chancellor's pre-budget report last Wednesday. They were left stunned, silent and in a terminal gloom as they struggled to retrieve some ground.

LESSONS from the US in democracy. The country which strides the globe as the true defender of democracy is learning:

If every vote counts, then you have to count every vote.[3]

14th November 2000

[1]   *UK National Audit Office Report, The Millennium Dome, published 8th November 2000.*
[2]   *Chancellor Gordon Brown delivered his "mini-Budget" on Wednesday 8th November 2000 which gave extra funding to pensioners and motorists. Mr Brown announced a freeze in fuel duty and a cut of 3p per litre in "green" ultra-low sulphur petrol (ULSP) and diesel. For the single pensioner there was a proposed future cash increase of £5-a-week and for a married couple a rise of £8-a-week. (Lower than that being proposed in the Liberal Democrat alternative budget!)*
[3]   *See Appendix, pp. 182-183*

Can do (what we tell you to do) culture

A NEW Parliamentary Session opens with a fresh Queen's Speech. As usual, fresh red carpets are rolled out and previously unreachable cobwebs are swept from the rafters. We all hope for a perceptible sign of the Queen's enthusiasm or disapproval for anything which she will read, but will, once again, be sorely disappointed.

But keen political lobbyists will not be listening for clues in the tone of the Queen's voice. The question will be whether the Prime Minister presents a short programme of 'popular' measures which will be a curtain raiser for a General Election in May or present a full list of Bills in a synthetic attempt to give an impression of a full session continuing up to November next year.

Whichever interpretation is put on it, if Cornwall and Scilly were to put a bid in for its own 'Queen's Speech' there are a number of measures we would be pressing for (irrespective of which political party were in control).

AN EQUITY of Funding Bill would clearly be a high priority for us. On the two key 'totem' areas of public expenditure—health and education—Cornwall receives significantly less than the average for England and Wales. £96 per head of population less than the average spending on health and £100 per Cornish school child less than the average for education. Considering our particular geographical challenges this deserves special attention.

But there is another area which is already frustrating many of those seeking to make the critical change to Cornwall's future economic development. That is the complexity surrounding the administration of Cornwall's Objective One status. The reality of any Government matched funds is an opportunity to be strangled in red tape in pursuit of small pots of money with a forest of strings attached.

In fact Cornwall's and the Scilly's attempt to make the most of European Structural Funds is a contradiction to the advice often given.

In the lead up to the implementation of Cornwall's Objective One programme we were encouraged by Government Departments, agencies and experts to throw off the shackles of low esteem and mounting negativity to establish a new "can do" culture.

Those who have tried to make the Objective One programme work for Cornwall and Scilly are complaining that the Government Offices and Departments are adding new regulations with every passing day.

The "can do" culture appears to have been reinterpreted in certain Government and regional quango circles as "can do…what we tell you to do!"

Whether "cultures" and "attitudes" can be legislated for or simply fought for is no doubt a matter for debate.

ONE THING IS LIKELY from a Parliamentary Session which is anticipated to be stopped short in the Spring of next year. That is that little of what Parliament will have to debate in the coming months will have any consequence on legislation as Parliament will have to start the whole process over again when a new Parliament is elected.

The goal of challenging "control freak cultures" in the regional quangos in achieving small but significant victories for Cornwall has to be our priority, rather than getting bogged down in a legislative process which is largely destined to grind into the dust.

However, a once lonely furrow I have been ploughing for some time did bear fruit last week when, in the Government's Rural Areas White Paper[1], the Deputy Prime Minister agreed to consult on a proposal to remove the 50% Council Tax discount for second home owners. Previously, I have been told on many occasions that I was wasting my time and that it would never be done only to find those same critics claiming their own personal victories among the spoils of this mini triumph.

Politics continues to be a revealing zoo of human nature.

5th December 2000

[1] *The Government's Rural White Paper "Our Countryside: The Future—A Fair Deal for Rural England" was published on 28th November 2000. Andrew George had raised the matter of the 50% Council Tax rebate many times with Government Ministers through letters, meetings, Parliamentary Questions and, significantly, in a debate he called with local Government Minister, Chris Mullin MP, on 9th February 2000.*

Nadelek Lowen

IN THE USA it is not just "dimpled chads"[1] which have been feeling rejected: last week, small children were in tears when they witnessed Father Christmas being arrested in a department store in New York. Allegedly Santa—as the Yanks prefer to call him—had got into a brawl with a young man and was marched off by the police.

I am reliably informed that this was not the real Father Christmas, so children can sleep happily in their beds this Christmas. Phew…

MORE NEWS: People in West Cornwall have been celebrating after more than a day without rain. But don't worry, they should have the standpipes out by the end of the weekend.

Usually, this level of cynicism is merely saved for politicians and others in public service. Fortunately, despite every effort on the part of politicians to intervene in every aspect of people's lives it is quite clear that legislators, like myself, cannot legislate to make people have a happy Christmas. We cannot even legislate to put a smile on the face of any modern day Scrooge.

But we can attempt to legislate to help make Christmas less sad, uncomfortable or lonely for those who are getting a raw deal out of life.

We still haven't got it right. I doubt that we will ever get close to the utopia some of us dream of. But we must always strive towards achieving the best possible settlement for all.

Christmas is, quite rightly, a time when many of those who know they are going to have a good time stop and think and act for those for whom Christmas will not really be an occasion to celebrate. But while you are rightly considering what you can do for those less fortunate than yourselves, don't forget to put aside some time to celebrate yourself.

Nadelek Lowen ba Blethen Noweth da.
I wish all residents in West Cornwall and the Isles of Scilly a very Merry Christmas and a Happy New Year.

18th December 2000

[1]   *"Dimpled chads" are the incompletely punched holes which were uncounted in Florida and a cause for argument and recrimination in the most wafer thin of US Presidential Election counts.*

Resolutely real

WELL, IT'S a New Year and now, after last year's false start, we have now entered the real New Millennium. It's a chance to turn a new leaf.

Perhaps we should all have a "New Millennium" resolution of truly millennial proportion. "End all war", "solve world hunger", "save the planet" might be some.

But our personal resolutions will be more modest. We probably all want to be a bit better, more successful and less worse as human beings.

Common sense tells us that true happiness and satisfaction is found in ensuring the shortest distance between ambition and reality or hope and inevitability. Resolving to get out of bed most mornings, put the dust bin out on collection day and empty the ash trays when full should, I hope, leave few with disappointment.

Yet, still we should all play our part in striving to live up to more ambitious goals which we should continually press our politicians and bankers, business people and charities to achieve—for the greater good.

While some political persuasions will try to entice us to join them in their quest for prejudice, intolerance and greed, millennial resolutions should challenge our selflessness towards others—for people we will never meet or know and for a future we will not have the opportunity to enjoy.

On their own, politicians can't end wars or stop world poverty etc. but, with strong popular support, the chance of getting closer to it improves dramatically.

Therefore, one of your New Year's resolutions (though I don't thank myself for suggesting it) should be: Keep politicians on their toes!

1st January 2001

Fishing in past waters

I **KNOW I HAVE** been a politician for a number of years now. But my transformation into an insensitive and unprincipled sleaze ball like all the others is evidently not yet complete. At times there are still disturbing signs of an ordinary human being trying to get out.

This week I wondered whether it would be possible to relive experiences of real human sensitivity thirty years on.

In, until now, a little reported batch of Cabinet memos released under the Thirty Year Rule confirmed the suspicions of many at the time that fishermen's interests would be "expendable" in order to meet the bigger goal of easing Britain into Europe.[1]

I well recollect sitting beside the former Prime Minister—Ted Heath MP—during the last annual fishing debate when he used his last opportunity for a Commons speech to attempt to correct criticisms made of him by others—including, more recently, his own Party—at the time of Britain's entry into the EU.

WHAT I BELIEVE the Cabinet memos reveal is that there were probably many matters going on at the time, which it would have been impossible for a Prime Minister to have kept tabs on. A Scottish Office paper at the time stated that in the wider interests of the UK British fishermen "must be regarded as expendable".

At the time, Scottish fishermen and those fishing in the North Sea came out of negotiations with a reasonable deal but Cornish fishermen were left with a poor share of the available quota. This agreement has provided a basis on which quotas have been divided up ever since and, even today, are a cause of deep irritation amongst Cornish fishermen in particular and the British industry in general.

On the assumption that the former Prime Minister was being candid with the House last year, it shows how much he was blanching from the criticism made of his efforts in the past. Though the revelation of the Cabinet Office memos may demonstrate that there were some matters kept from the attention of Ministers at the time.

Whether or not the Ministers and Mandarins involved now feel sensitive about something which took place thirty years ago is open to speculation. However, what we do know is that the fishing industry —especially in Cornwall—has good reason to feel sore about this thirty years on.

16th January 2001

[1]   *"Secret documents revealed…under the 30-year rule complete the story of the most cynical smash-and-grab raid in the history of the European Union.*
"It was this that led the prime minister of the day, Edward Heath, to give away the world's richest fishing waters—a national resource worth tens of billions of pounds—as the price he was prepared to pay to fulfil his dream of taking Britain into the Common Market in January 1973.
"…Heath's ministers…were prepared to lie openly to Parliament to hide what they had done." Christopher Booker's Notebook, The Daily Telegraph, 14th January 2001

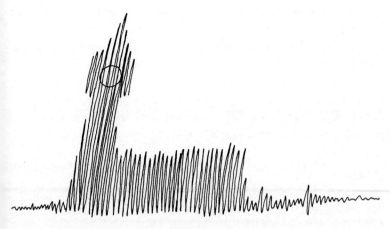

The Parliamentary Richter scale

THE HOUSE of Commons never looks more absurd than when it gets over excited about trivia.

The resignation/sacking of Peter Mandelson has set hares racing all over the Palace of Westminster.[1] It has woken some MPs up from their slumber and diverted them towards apparently purposeful activity.

A few questions from my Parliamentary colleague, Norman Baker MP[2], a week ago has sparked off a feeding frenzy of absurd proportions. For many, nothing else seems to matter.

A massive earthquake in Gujarat state, India[3], in which tens of thousands of people have been killed or are missing seems to have had little impact on the Richter Scale of the chattering classes who have become transfixed on who said what to who in a two minute telephone conversation years before.

They demand to know. They want answers. And they want them urgently. More urgently than getting help to the rescue teams in Bhuj.

The juvenile hysteria which is always bubbling just below the surface has the ability to mask serious concerns if petty mindedness erupts.

The frankly disturbing attitude of the new President of the United States towards foreign affairs should worry politicians here.[4] The US's potential to destabilise other parts of the world should be a matter for serious debate.

But to the obsessive gossip and rumour chaser it is of little importance. They now have a new lease of life, scurrying around corridors, getting into purposeful huddles and keeping the blood racing.

The big difference between rumours and innuendoes over a badly handled piece of casework and a major earthquake in which tens of thousands of people are killed is…you can't score tawdry political points about an earthquake.

30th January 2001

[1]   Peter Mandelson, then Northern Ireland Secretary resigned from Government on 24th January 2001 to fight claims that he had used his influence to obtain a passport for two Indian entrepreneurs GP and SP Hinduja, who had been major donors to the Millennium Dome when Mr Mandelson was Culture Secretary. The Hammond Report into the scandal, published in March 2001 argued that there was no reason to doubt Mr Mandelson's honesty and that he did not lie to Downing Street over his involvement.
[2]   Norman Baker, Liberal Democrat MP for the rural and normally safe Tory seat of Lewes (Sussex) was returned at the 2001 General Election with a majority of 9,710. It was as a result of his tenacious questioning that some of the apparent inconsistencies in this affair came to light.
[3]   On 26th January 2001 an earthquake measuring 7.9 on the Richter scale hit the Indian state of Gujarat, killing at least 30,000 people. The most devastated district was Kutch, with the epicentre occurring just outside its capital, Bhuj.
[4]   President George W Bush was sworn in as US President on 20th January 2001, already arguing for a National Defence Missile System, christened by many political pundits "Star Wars II".

Not all lovey-dovey

UNFORTUNATELY St Valentine hasn't brought on an outbreak of sweetness and light in Parliament this week. In fact, a hard frost fell upon the Palace of Westminster and Cupid took cover as the customary no-love-lost battles resumed in the Chamber.

A warming of relations would result in better, though less newsworthy, Government. From the viewpoint of those struggling to keep business afloat in West Cornwall and Scilly, this week brought evidence more of a contrary than a romantically agreeable nature.

● While our small family farmers struggle through their worst recession for more than a generation, agribusiness Barons in the east of England are given £1 million cheques of taxpayers' subsidy they don't need.

● While our fishermen, who now need investment more desperately than ever, struggle on hoping that stocks will recover, more than £55 million of UK taxpayers' money is paid to compensate foreign fishermen following the fiasco of ill advised legislation brought in by a previous government.[1]

● Weeks after oil companies sought sympathy for having to cope with high crude oil prices this week they reported raking in profits by the £billion.[2]

● Then in a debate I called this week we began to understand that too much Government intervention in West Cornwall was stifling rather than generating economic development[3].

Perhaps the political process is becoming more "wires crossed" than "star crossed".

13th February 2001

[1]   *Regarding the "Factortame" case and the resulting compensation to "flag of convenience" vessels which were illegally removed from the British register following the 1988 Merchant Shipping Act.*
[2]   *Shell, Europe's largest oil company, announced on 8th February 2001 an 85% increase in annual profits to £9.4bn—a profit rate equivalent to more than £1m an hour.*
[3]   *Debate on Regional Economic Development, Westminster Hall, 13th February 2001, Column 1WH.*

Contaminated thoughts

YOU CAN ALWAYS tell when Parliament demonstrates how irrelevant it is. Speakers quickly resort to pitiful jibes.

So this week, dealing with the seriousness of the spreading Foot and Mouth epidemic[1], members were able to "amaze" with their own variations on the "Foot in Mouth" accusation against anyone they disagree with. The audible groans have become expressions of undiluted pain.

So the Foot and Mouth crisis has exposed a brand new political crisis which may result in the postponement of the General Election, which had been expected imminently. Time is now needed to allow Party managers the opportunity to sack script-writers as politicians find themselves stuck on the "Foot in Mouth" record.

Spin doctors clearly hadn't prepared their front line fighters for this. Those boys and girls on the front line are still in point-scoring mode, but unable to jump on passing bandwagons which are disinfected against political contamination.

MEANWHILE senior Whips look on enviously as Ministry vets are given permission to create pyres of carcasses of unwanted beasts they believe are good for nothing else.

The plot of spin doctors and whips to stun the back bench lobby fodder into a state of continual "manic exaltation of the leader and all his great works"[2] can sometimes be contaminated by the contagion of independent thought.

Once it takes hold it can sometimes spread rapidly and many of those who have become infected never fully recover...

27th February 2001

[1]   *The first outbreak of Foot and Mouth Disease in Britain since 1967 was confirmed on 20th February 2001.*
[2]   *Quoted from Paul Flynn MP "Commons Knowledge" (p. 140)*

The Big Idea

WE ARE ABOUT to enter a new political season. It is just as absurd as it is inescapable.

It is a season in which those politicians who take themselves far too seriously collude with political commentators.

Because it is almost the time in the political calendar when political leaders launch **"The Big Idea"**. Politicians—especially political leaders—are expected to have one. Being caught in possession without one is considered to be a sign of political failure.

Whether it be "promoting the free market", "socialism", "capitalism", "saving Britain from becoming a foreign land", "the social market", "the Third Way" or merely "(insert Leader's name)-ism", **The Big Idea** must apply in all aspects of life, no matter the circumstances. It is sometimes acceptable for **The Big Idea** to be, in fact, an old idea, but repackaged.

The launch of **The Big Idea** has to catch the popular imagination.

The Big Idea has to be presented as an event in which the political Leader has been suddenly and uniquely struck by a blinding flash of the obvious. It has to be a solution which has strangely bypassed the whole of the human race for centuries before.

You might think that all politicians in Westminster now have time for little else than striking up Rodin's classic pose of great thinkers (hand to forehead, elbow to knee) caught in the most arduous cerebral effort. Perhaps others might be scouring the land for the political equivalent of the Holy Grail.

WHILE I have been doing both of course I have been thinking a lot about how all of the nations—nay, the world's—problems could be solved in one simplistic concept. This is the "irreducible minimum"; durable in all conditions.

It has taken much effort on my part and, exclusively for readers of *The Cornishman* I have decided to unveil my very own **Big Idea** on an awestruck public. This is it:

Beware people with Big Ideas.

I hope you like it. It may catch on!

The big problem with **Big Ideas** is that the problems of the world are too varied and too complex for simple resolution. People who promote a blind faith in **Big Ideas** may get a bit too big for their boots.

I prefer many and varied ideas—even if, on occasions, they seem contradictory.

13th March 2001

141

Contagious virus strikes Westminster

VETS, SLAUGHTERMEN and the armed forces are on standby in Westminster. But the vast majority of MPs seem blissfully unaware of the danger in their midst.

No one seems to know where the infection came from. Some swear that it was illegally imported and others claim that it was contracted from a Lobby journalist desperate for a new angle on the Foot and Mouth disease now gripping the countryside.[1]

Wherever it came from, one thing is sure. This nasty little virus is proving very contagious. Outbreaks of "Benefit of Hindsight Disease" (or BHD) are emerging all over both Houses of Parliament.

UNLIKE Foot and Mouth it has a relatively short incubation period. Measured rational judgements can suddenly be cast aside. Previous pronouncements that Ministers have got their full backing, that they would have done nothing different, that they accept that the Foot and Mouth crisis is a biological rather than political challenge can evaporate instantaneously. A form of pre-election nervosa can weaken their resolve and they become more susceptible to the disease.

The main symptoms are a brass neck and short-term memory.

For example in the recent Foot and Mouth crisis people who contracted this awful and debilitating disease said nothing other than agree that actions taken were the right ones. Yet, as soon as the Benefit of Hindsight virus strikes them, the world can suddenly be seen through different eyes. To them it is obvious that the Army should have been brought in earlier, contingency plans should have been in place long ago, Ministers should have anticipated this happening, help should have been made available earlier. To them it is quite clear that, had they been in control of the crisis, the Foot and Mouth virus would have retired early and gone somewhere rather than face such a concerted onslaught.

It hasn't caught everyone just yet. The slaughtermen are ready for the cull.

27th March 2001

[1]   *By midday on 27th March 2001 there had been 649 cases of Foot and Mouth Disease confirmed.*

Sentence deferred

AS WESTMINSTER breaks for a busy Easter recess many MPs will be breathing a sigh of relief at their temporary freeing from "death row". Many MPs simply want to get it over and done with. Others demonstrate signs of relief at a death sentence deferred.[1]

But it is not so much certain death as the predictable "duffing up" we all have to endure at the hands of an intimidating electorate every 4 years or so.

Politicians are often seen as suitable receptacles on which the electorate can happily or angrily unburden all their troubles and disappointments with a heavy dose of personal blame attached.

In the league tables of professional esteem politicians generally feature some way below estate agents, mass murderers and fraudsters.

Rats are the animal kingdom's equivalent of politicians—deeply uncuddly, verminous and an all-round public relations disaster.

During elections MPs will have doors slammed in their faces and be told, "Oh, you're all as bad as each other", "I wouldn't trust you lot as far as I could throw you" and the rest of the usual stuff.

Certainly politicians are amongst the least impressive of human beings. Eager to please, it is believed that there can be no limits to their insincerity.

So electors conclude: "We'd be better off without you all" or "We should get rid of the lot of you."

THOUGH I can sympathise with this understandable gut instinct the question often has to be asked, "Well, what would you put in our place?"

Unless we were happy to have a dictatorship or an absolute monarchy we would still need people to decide how much tax we should pay and how to fund public services; how and when to deploy the army in a crisis; and who should and should not receive the support of taxpayers' money and so on.

You could select the most popular and glamorous stars to make these decisions but unpopular decisions could not be avoided. A Government run by Posh and Becks, Branson, Geldoff, Hollywood stars and the benefit of hindsight political commentators, would stil have to learn that there are limits to time, money, and patience where decisions are being taken.

In justifying themselves and seeking a continued mandate they would end up behaving…well, just like politicians.

I don't know whether politicians are selectively bred to have the thick skins they need to cope with the lampooning or whether a survival instinct keeps us all going.

Electors may grudgingly vote for the least worst of all options and politicians may survive the baiting and tormenting but at the end of the day no one has yet come up with a better system.

10th April 2001

[1]   On 2nd April 2001 the Prime Minister officially postponed the local elections due to take place on 3rd May until 7th June. This also ended months of speculation about a 3rd May General Election.

Mongrels of the world unite

I HAD GONE into the House of Commons Tea Room for a mug of cocoa at the end of a late night sitting.

I was chatting to a group of fellow political "mongrels"[1]—most of us proudly claim to have real human being blood in us!—when the subject turned to the vexed question of race and identity. I was sitting opposite colleagues mostly from Scotland. I offered the following observation:

"Of course the Scots need the English to help define who they are, and the Welsh are not that fond of the English either.

"The English don't know who they are and usually mutter something about cricket—which they are not very good at anyway.

"Whereas the Cornish are modest and kind and love you all without exception!"

There was an interesting silence, while my Scottish colleagues quietly smouldered.

"What, even the Devonians?" ventured one.

"Well, we just feel sorry for them. What with Foot and Mouth and not being as good at most things as we are," I replied.

I am sure that some of us were feeling tired and emotional but despite the late hour, there were no ugly incidents. The banter was good humoured.

It is good to have pride in who we are, an attachment to place and a sense of strength from the group of people we identify with. We should celebrate the diversity of communities, identities, ethnic and racial groups. Fortunately the spirit of people is stronger than politicians and their prejudices.

THE MOST cowardly of politicians are those who so fear opposition to their views amongst voters in this country, that they seek to make enemies of those who cannot vote against them—"foreigners", asylum seekers, other European nations, etc.

Those who seem to believe that there are votes in uniting the people of this country in opposition to people who are *not* of this country have, thankfully, been ridiculed and ultimately defeated.

Britain is a welcoming and accommodating country. There is little evidence to suggest that we are "thoroughbreds" rather than "mongrels".

This is especially the case in Cornwall, which has historically been less "insular" than most other parts of the UK (largely as a result of its maritime heritage and poverty which has often resulted in mass emigration to other parts of the world).

Although we are quite used to being simultaneously accused of being both "inbred" and "not existing", the people who have come and gone or stayed have, more often than not, had a big heart and a broad vision.

Cornwall, just like Britain, should cut itself into the celebration of diversity. Not seek to cut itself off from the rest of the world.

1st May 2001

[1]   *On 30th April 2001 East Yorkshire MP—John Townend—created a political stir and great offence by implying that there were too many black and Asian people in Britain and after commenting that the British are in danger of becoming a "mongrel race". The adverse publicity resulted in William Hague allegedly reprimanding him.*

Old lessons for a new Parliament

WITH ALMOST two cheers ringing in our ears the new House of Commons happily assembled last week (most normal folk now perceive us as having marginally more legitimacy than the House of Lords).[1]

The nearly 100 new members will have many lessons to learn quickly. Here are just three of them:

THE FIRST is that they must behave as if they have had magical powers bestowed upon them.

The most obvious is to have learned how to "walk on water".[2] Most MPs quickly realise that complete or even blissful ignorance normally provides no bar to the average backbencher fulfilling his/her daily routine of pontificating on a stream of complex matters. Some describe it as "treading on a sea of bull****". The risk of becoming submerged is ever present.

The public often ask how unexceptional mortals operate as walking encyclopaedias, daily preaching on thermodynamics, jurisprudence, social security law, third world debt, human rights in Turkmenistan, stem cell research and fibre optic cabling. But asking questions like that is like "skating on thin ice".

THE SECOND lesson will be to find out whether Parliament is merely a tool for rubber-stamping the desire of Government or that it has another role.

There are two ways in which a Government can take Parliament for granted. The first is to have enough Government backbenchers who are prepared to lie back and empty their minds of troublesome thoughts.

And the other is to have an opposition which sees its role solely in terms of hovering around waiting to seize on failure or a passing bandwagon of opportunity.

Challenging the government with robust debate on the basis of a genuine intention and commitment to get things right is rare.

THE THIRD lesson is to discover which end of the "them and us" telescope you side with. Does Whitehall really know best or are people in London out of touch?

147

If you were a head teacher drowning under the routine tidal wave of initiatives, circulars and dictats or you are a community unable to take the simplest decision for yourselves you may have a view on this.

But for the unwary MP, Westminster has the capacity to seduce you into believing what all centralised remote managers believe about their own infallibility. That anyone who is not themselves is obviously incompetent and has no initiative—unless and until they can prove otherwise.

So, beware!

26th June 2001

[1]   *The General Election took place on June 7th. Labour were returned to Government with a majority of 165. The Liberal Democrats lost two seats but gained 7 to become the third largest Party in British history and the Tories returned 166 MPs compared to 165 in 1997. Andrew George was returned with an increased majority (from 7,170 to 10,053 on a turnout which fell by 8.8%), taking 51.6% of the vote; giving him the largest parliamentary majority in Cornwall.*
[2]   *Paul Flynn, "Commons Knowledge: How to be a Backbencher", 1997 (p. 146).*

Pipers calling the tune

SIFTING THROUGH the debris of another week in Parliament it is difficult not to come to the conclusion that the place is just as predictable as ever.

While the main opposition party remains obsessed with frantically rearranging the deckchairs on its titanic "flag of convenience" vessel[1], the Government still seeks to make a virtue of not being "Socialist".

And Lobby journalists have been handed the "story of the week" on a plate when they could see MPs nosediving into the trough without blindfolds.

No doubt the Tory leadership contest will throw up some intrigue, but they might hope that the leadership contest lasts until the next General Election—thus giving them almost total media domination, without having to discuss policy in anything other than terms of the need for a "review".

Other parties are no doubt hoping that the longer the leadership contest goes on, the shorter will be the "honeymoon" for the new leader after all the dust has settled.

MEANWHILE, this week's announcement—needless to say not to Parliament—that the Government intends to introduce new three-year tests for those longer term disabled on Incapacity Benefit[2] will add to the ill health of many.

Letting slip that they believe that up to 70% of those people currently in receipt of this benefit are capable of some work suggests that the Benefits Agency may be setting new "targets" rather than an objective test to cut out fraud from the system. Whether the proposed tests will merely create more ill health, or save the taxpayer money will depend on what the Government's real intention is—we will have a chance to see when they have the confidence to actually bring the proposal to Parliament itself.

In contrast, the image every three or four years, of MPs voting themselves another pay rise above inflation, will have a reassuring feel for all those heartily cynical of all politicians. My (and others') attempts to link all future pay settlements with nurses', teachers' and other public sector workers' pay review bodies failed to win sufficient support, as contorted logic won the day.[3]

Although this merely brings us back to where we were four years ago it is quite clear that MPs must establish a basis on which to detach themselves from the "Railtrack"[4] scenario of generous rewards despite public opinion and performance.

I wonder what we would be paid if we left it to ordinary taxpayers to decide?

10th July 2001

[1]   On 10th July 2001 five candidates stood in the first ballot of Conservative MPs for the Party Leadership: Michael Portillo, Michael Ancram, Kenneth Clarke, Iain Duncan Smith and David Davis. Portillo won with 49 votes, Duncan Smith came second with 39 votes, Clarke received 36 votes and Ancram and Davis tied in last place with 21 votes.

[2]   In early July 2001 the Prime Minister Tony Blair vowed to push through changes to the benefits system which would see disabled people undergo medicals to check whether they are fit for work. He faced strong criticism in the Commons from many MPs and disability campaigners over what they called "MoT tests" for the sick and vulnerable.

[3]   Against the Government backed motion Chris Mullin—MP for Sunderland South—argued that MPs' pay should rise in line with average increases in the public sector. Andrew George supported Chris Mullin's amendment.

[4]   On 21st June 2001 a £1.4m pay-off was awarded to Gerald Corbett, the former Chief Executive of Railtrack who had originally offered his resignation after four people died in the Hatfield rail crash in November 2000.

Holding Ministers and criminals to account

A GOOD and bad week for Westminster politicians.

GOOD: A successful uprising against Government Whips has improved the chance of Parliament actually holding the Government and Government Ministers to account.[1]

Therefore a bad week for Ministers who treat Parliament as a rubber stamping chamber they can largely take for granted.

"Select" Committees sound rather exclusive, but they can present Government Ministers with the maximum opportunity for embarrassment and the closest scrutiny of those aspects of their work they would rather leave unscrutinised. I have served on one—Agriculture[2]—and am awaiting confirmation of my appointment to another—Regional Affairs.

Of course, Select Committees will often have members from the Government's benches who loyally swallow the spoon-fed syrupy reassurances of their Party's senior colleagues but, in the main, experience suggests that divisions within those committees are not always on Party lines. Select Committees provide the best opportunity for genuine scrutiny and independent thought and the decision of Parliament to tell the Whips that appointments to those committees are the prerogative of Parliament and not of Government is the most welcome piece of news for a very long time for those who like to watch closely the activities of Westminster.

BAD: Yes, a bad week for those politicians who fear that we will all be tarred by the same brush as that which has just given former Conservative MP and Party Vice Chairman Lord Archer a good dousing this week.[3]

Some constituents see Jeffrey Archer merely as one who considers himself unlucky enough to have been caught and, until he shows serious signs of contrition, merely helps to promote that impression.

I don't know whether, like Jonathan Aitken (the last senior figure from the high water mark of the Thatcher years to "fall"), he will "find God", apparent forgiveness and a promise of a future life in sackcloth and ashes.

I suspect that politicians will simply have to accept the fact that the majority see us as "all the same"!

GOOD: And a good week for House of Commons staff who have now seen MPs go off to their constituencies for the summer recess. The majority of MPs, of course, will be diligently concentrating on constituency work and preparing for the next parliamentary session; though many will leave the bulk of that to their overworked staff while they escape for weeks on end.

24th July 2001

[1]   *Hansard, 16th July 2001, Column 77 ff.*
[2]   *Agriculture Select Committee from 1997-2000; Regional Affairs Committee—*
appointed before the General Election of 2001 and since confirmed.
[3]   *On 19th July 2001 Jeffrey Archer was sentenced to four years imprisonment for*
lying by creating a false alibi during his 1987 trial against The Daily Star newspaper.

Far from the madding Westminster village

THERE WERE times during the winter when—with flooding, the wrong kind of politics on the line and serious accidents on the main roads—England, and London in particular, had become almost cut off from Cornwall.

Our normal mild concern about the geographical remoteness and intellectual isolation of London and the South East arose, not just when Foot and Mouth disease struck the country but when a parallel and debilitating human disease gripped Westminster.

I refer, of course, to the "Benefit of Hindsight Disease". The symptoms of short-term memory loss and a brass neck were evident to all who managed to keep clear of it.

In contrast, here in Cornwall and on the Isles of Scilly, we recognise that most normal folk need a break from the intoxicating pastimes of either bandwagon leaping or swallowing spoon-fed syrupy reassurances.

However, an escape from the intensely parochial environs of Westminster to a place which—despite every attempt to homogenise the UK—remains one of the most distinctive places on these islands would be a smart move. But perhaps that depends on which end of the "them and us" telescope you believe you are looking into.

The West Cornwall and Isles of Scilly holiday "pledge card" doesn't include the guarantee of wall to wall sunshine on every single day, though we invariably enjoy a late summer in September and October, when most of the rest of the country is already counting down the shopping days to Christmas.

Nor—despite our distinctiveness—do we offer a "Balkan" holiday, with its attendant ethnic cleansing of English folk. In fact, we are very welcoming, really.

West Cornwall and the Isles of Scilly is the very best place to enjoy your holiday. My own constituency offers a wealth of good quality and tasteful activities and Theme Parks for families, many fascinating local museums and sumptuous art galleries, a geological museum, Trinity House Museum, 2 tin mines, country walks, coastal walks, miles and miles of golden sand for many weary paunches to rest, invigorating sea and surf overlooked by lifeguards, good quality restaurants, gardens, boat trips, fishing trips, helicopter and plane trips. Or you can always enjoy the increasingly popular spectator sport of watching the local MP being harangued by his constituents at various villages, towns and islands around the constituency at publicly advertised times during September and October. With the possible demise of the two local fox hunts, this new sport has potential for the particularly bloodthirsty.

By then, if you haven't met the Cornish folk in our social housing reservations or as quaint appendages to the romantic landscape, you can see how we used to live at the many Celtic settlements, stone circles and burial chambers scattered mainly around the Penwith moors, but also on The Lizard and the Scillies.

Although I do not operate as a tourist office, I can and am prepared to offer advice for those prepared to take the risk of contacting me.

Have a great Holiday.

6th August 2001

Cheap food leading to ranch and prairie

JUST WHEN we thought it was safe to venture back out into the countryside, farming is being hit by yet another devastating disease. It could see half of all our farms wiped out within the next twenty years.

As if farming hasn't already suffered enough, the Government appears to have created their very own and particularly devastating strain of virus, one which has previously threatened the industry.

Worse than BSE and FMD, this disease can affect not just cloven hooved animals.

The Scapegoat Small farmers Disease (or SSD) has been lying dormant in a Government laboratory until its release this week when the Prime Minister announced the appointment of Lord Haskins as his very own "Rural Recovery" co-ordinator—a contradiction in terms if ever I have seen one.

His brief will cover the whole of the rural economy including tourism, small businesses and farming but he has yet to make the connection between the lack of countryside visits in areas of extensive ranches and prairies.

Lord Haskins, who is Chairman of Northern Foods and a Labour Peer, is known to be fiercely critical of small farms and also of agricultural subsidies. His primary claim is that small farms are particularly culpable of inefficiency, taking more than their fair share of subsidies and are less environmentally friendly than larger farms.

A fortnight ago he predicted that "farms will get bigger and that's a good thing".

ALL THIS comes at a time when it has emerged that the Foot and Mouth crisis has created 37 farming millionaires—i.e. farmers who have made compensation claims totalling more than £1 million. One farmer is set to receive £4.2 million in compensation. The total cost of the slaughter policy could eventually cost the taxpayer as much as £5 billion (the equivalent of at least 2 pence on income tax); higher than the cost of the BSE outbreak.

But let's get a few things straight here. Of course farmers have been criticised for being "mollycoddled" by subsidies and it is true that they take half of the E.U. expenditure. That needs to change.

And the farming industry has been rightly criticised for failing to accept that there is generally a climate for fraud created by these subsidies—both in other European countries as well as our own.

However, to suggest that small farmers are uniquely culpable is wrong. Large farmers do especially well out of a system based on production and volume.

Call me sentimental if you like, but I don't happen to believe that small farmers are the villains in all this. I suppose I'm biased because of my small farming background but I remember the essential contribution locally based small family farms have always played in the local community, the local economy and how sensitive many have been to their local heritage and ecology.

Though that's not always the case small farms, which are part of their local scene, have generally been less damaging to the environment than larger ones.

This was spelt out to me when I worked in agriculture and development work in Nottinghamshire. On the first day I arrived one parish council was complaining about an agribusiness take over of three small farms and which turned them into a single field over one weekend! Hopefully this will never happen in Cornwall.

If Lord Haskins is happy to see the countryside turned into a cheap food production base of prairie and ranch I suspect he may have a fight on his hands.

7th August 2001

Rearranging the deck chairs

SPARE a thought for Opposition Parties.

While the governing Party quietly gets on with the job of Government, the focus is being switched to Opposition Parties, and the Conservatives in particular, who will soon decide whether they can produce a Leader worth voting for.

Only two years ago we Liberal Democrats went through the same process ourselves. Therefore, broadly speaking, my thoughts on this apply whatever the Opposition Party.

Basically, an Opposition Party has to decide whether it has the capacity to look outwards, or is so concerned about its internal debates that it can only look inwards.

Making an Opposition Party relevant to a wider public, rather than a narrow membership, is perhaps the biggest challenge.

After all, what is the point of an Opposition Party?

IN A COUNTRY run by dictatorship, opposition movements are essential to galvanise hope, but in a democracy it has to be about more than simply providing a happy home for the knee jerk "No" camp. An Opposition Party is there to oppose Government effectively —not simply to be opportunistic and jump on passing bandwagons not of their creation and to oppose for opposition's sake.

But being an Opposition Party is also about presenting a positive agenda for a "better" life—not just a "less bad" one.

Being in Opposition is not necessarily something a political party aspires to become! Though it can sometimes seem like a terminal condition, there really is little to be gained from years in the political wilderness—unless you take the artistic view that it provides fertile ground for doleful, poetic reflection.

The challenge to a political opposition engaged in a leadership election is to turn public attention into public advantage and not let it become an embarrassing window on a private squabble. To the average Fred Trebloggs the whole process can appear like stumbling upon private bickering within an irrelevant debating society.

An Opposition Party has to settle its scores in private and to present to the public a force which can really challenge and cajole Government for the good.

Otherwise, whether it be Leadership elections or other internal debates it can prove to be little more than rearranging the deck chairs on a political Titanic.

Perhaps this is why the Conservative's Foreign Affairs Spokesman, Francis Maude, was hardly exaggerating this week when he described the Leadership contest as "a battle not only for the soul of his Party, but for its very survival".

21st August 2001

Nothing succeeds like failure

THERE STILL appears to be "one law for the rich…", as we hear that another Captain of Industry is rewarded for abject failure.

In a mere five years, Lord Simpson has helped to transform Marconi plc from one of British Industry's greatest successes into one of its most calamitous failures. This week, as the company confirmed that it is facing a £5bn loss this year, its Chief Executive, Lord Simpson, has baled out with an additional £1m pay-off, presumably in recognition of his achievements for the company.

As he left, Marconi the company was worth a mere 3% of what it was a year ago.

Perhaps the pay-off was for showing 10,000 of its blameless workers the door?

In a week when the Government is being held to account for planning to introduce private sector disciplines into our hospitals and schools, etc., it is worth reflecting on news from Marconi that where the workforce suffer the consequences for executive failure, rewards are still handed around in the Boardroom.

I HAD BEEN keeping in contact with Marconi plc over the last year with regard to its involvement in the Marconi Centenary celebrations in the village of my birth at Mullion in December this year. News that the company which bears the great inventor's name has sunk so ignominiously low does not help us to promote what should otherwise be an opportunity for genuine celebration.

But to be fair, it is not just the private sector which can achieve outstanding failure. Successive Governments which have brought us such notable financial black holes as the Millennium Dome and the Jubilee Line extension prefer to switch attention away from failure through forcing competitive tendering or "better value" auditing on local authorities.

THE CHIEF Executive of the Isles of Scilly Council—Philip Hygate —has complained to me that the Best Value audit for a number of services for the Council of the Isles of Scilly is actually "surreal", as the cost of the audit threatens to exceed the cost of providing the service!

And if that weren't enough, MPs are capable of monumental failure too. Though I am pleased I wasn't around at the time the decision was made, Portcullis House—part of the House of Commons—was opened publicly less than a year ago at the cost of £230m (just £80m over budget). But this week, it emerged that the building is now beginning to tilt. Whether it is tilting to the right or the left, no one is prepared to say and I wouldn't know because I don't have an office there. But two huge cranes have now been inserted in the middle of the building in an attempt to rectify the problem.

There was speculation during the heat of summer, when the building's air-conditioning system failed, that it was presumably going to win an architectural award!

Perhaps we have all become too cynical and should now begin challenging a culture which brazenly believes that "nothing succeeds like failure".

11th September 2001

The overwhelming retaliation of friendship

I HAVE TO say that it is with a little guilt and plenty of shame that I find myself adding to the column yards of news print following the appalling events in the US last week. Perhaps the acres of commentary and speculation, the wall-to-wall television and radio coverage are part of the inevitable attempt by us all to try and make sense of the seemingly senseless.[1]

As a politician, of course, it is my job to attempt to contribute to the policy framework in which this kind of event has happened. We must also work, above all, to avoid it happening again and an effective response should be agreed and carried out.

I WELL remember joining a handful of fellow MPs in a secure bunker in the Ministry of Defence in Whitehall when we were discussing a variety of threatening scenarios three years ago at the commencement of the Strategic Defence Review. There was general agreement that the most likely threat to the security of the West was to come from a handful of terrorists perpetrating an outrage by biological, chemical or other means. This was considered to be so out of kilter with the concept of "conventional" defence that it was assumed to be a matter for the Home Office and not Foreign Affairs and Defence strategies.

But the challenge now is to demonstrate absolute steely determination and cast-iron resolve to face down terror of the type witnessed last week.

That does not necessarily mean seeking the satisfaction of revenge or disproportionate retaliation.

From the snatches of news reporting, some of the most poignant and desperate cell phone calls in this modern age, the indelible and lingering memories were of love and not hate or a passionate demand for retaliation.

WE ALL KNOW that truth is supposed to be the first casualty of any war, but a considered, intelligent and effective response will be the second casualty if the blood curdling demands to wreak satisfaction are given credence.

A disproportionate response would see us all walk straight into a trap of escalating retaliations which foresight says is waiting for us.

In this space before the first response—and a response has to come —we have a golden opportunity to isolate our enemies and honour the dead by demonstrating our humanity.

If we make enemies of those who happen to share the same religious faith as the insane murderers we will succeed only in creating fertile territory for new generations of suicide bombers. The perpetrators of this evil were united only in one faith—overwhelming and obsessive hatred, not Islam. Making orphans of innocent Muslims in another land will only sow more seeds for future retaliation and so-called "martyrdom".

NOW IS THE TIME for those with real character, determination, leadership and cast-iron resolve to demonstrate their true strength. The West must gird its loins for the onslaught. The retaliation must be overwhelming and the strategy must be to work towards a world in which the West finds common cause with the vast majority of sane, moderate and reasonable Muslims and Islamic states. Only in this way can we isolate the handful of psychotic and vengeful terrorists who hide behind the cloak of religion as a means of giving credence to their terror campaigns.

18th September 2001

[1]   11th September 2001 will be a date etched on the memory of many in the world. Four internal US flights were hijacked by terrorists and flown into the twin towers of the World Trade Center, the Defence Department at the Pentagon and the fourth crash-landed in Pennsylvania. At least 7,000 people were estimated to have lost their lives in the Terrorist attacks. On the day of these tragic events most commentators are already assuming the guilt of Osama bin Laden, the fundamentalist Islamic Leader of the Al Q'aeda Terrorist Group who was living under the protectorate of the Taliban regime in Afghanistan.

Among the hundreds of heroes who gave their lives in order to save the lives of others was Vietnam War Veteran Rick Rescorla from Hayle (where Andrew George lives) in the St Ives Constituency and who is credited with saving thousands of people by calmly ushering them to safety from the South Tower where Mr Rescorla was a security guard. He was reported to have sung "Going up Camborne Hill coming down" as he guided people down the stairs.

Decisively cautious

ONE OF THE first rules of political survival is always to be decisive. "He who hesitates is lost" applies more to politics than possibly any other trade. Common perception suggests that indecisiveness is a clear sign of weakness.

But there is rarely an opportunity in the frenetic world of political posturing to consider whether caution is preferable to being decisive—if there is a prospect that you will be decisively wrong.

A decisive President might have flattened Kabul on the evening of 11th September. And although I don't doubt that many in the Western world would have understood what drove such a President to retaliate in that way, most now, with the benefit of reflective caution, would acknowledge that this would have been a wrong move.

"THE SLAUGHTER of so many unsuspecting innocent people in so few hours surely has no peace time parallel. No declaration of war, no warning, no demands preceding it, and no claim of responsibility following it. To call these horrors the gravest mass murder and conspiracy ever to have occurred in peace time is inadequate".

"While we all still struggle to express our shock and sympathy, time is passing and, we hope, blind retaliation is slowing being taken off the agenda. But the twofold mission to find and punish the guilty and to prevent further terrorist attack is vitally urgent".[2]

Perhaps it is now worth reflecting upon not only the human cost of war but the financial cost as well.

The Gulf War (1990-1991) cost $61.1 billion of which the allied coalition reimbursed the US for 88% (around $54 billion).

Every cruise missile launch can cost over $2 million apiece and we know that Merlin Helicopters come for more than £40 million each.

LAST WEEK, the UN Emergency Relief Co-ordinator, Kenzo Oshima, told us that "Afghanistan is the site of the world's worst humanitarian crisis". On the same day the UN launched a formal appeal for $500 million (£340 million) to deal with up to 1.5 million new refugees and the 3.5 million Afghans already in camps in Pakistan and Iran.

In contrast to the millions of refugees who have been accepted in

Pakistan and Iran, Britain last year granted asylum to a mere 10,185 asylum seekers. 76,850 were refused.

The way to build bridges between the rich West and these poor Muslim states is to support the people and not bomb them.

Many people are now talking about the present situation as a "golden opportunity" to turn over a new leaf in our shared foreign and defence policies.

Though, for some, it will smack of indecision, showing restraint and humanity will be the smartest and most decisive thing we can do.[1]

2nd October 2001

---

[1]   *The US-led bombing of military and terrorist targets in Afghanistan commenced on the evening of Sunday 7th October. Although Andrew George acknowledged that the weight of evidence overwhelmingly pointed to the guilt of Bin Laden, he was unconvinced that the bombing should have commenced as soon as it did. More time should have been given to aid the humanitarian effort in support of the Afghan people.*

[2]   *As quoted from Liberal Democrat Lawyers' magazine for October 2001*

Gravy train stopped in its tracks

AS IF WE didn't know all along, now it has become official. Government departments behave just like corporations, groups and normal people, and would generally prefer to release less popular news at a time when we're all preoccupied with something else than let it explode into the middle of a news drought.

The, perhaps hapless (or unlucky) Civil Servant, Jo Moore, who's infamous email advising colleagues at the time of the strikes on the World Trade Center, that "it's a very good day" to bury bad news has made her a household name around the country and suitable weapon in the Commons this week.[1]

Those righteous members who gleefully thrust an image of Jo Moore in the faces of everyone else must have serious problems at meal times when butter fails to melt in their mouths. But, of course, that old thing called "human nature" should make us less gullible.

We all "proclaim bright triumphs from the rooftops and slip out the garbage via the backdoor" (Peter Preston in *The Guardian* this week).

Except there is no law which says that unused information from one day cannot be revealed when time and space permits. Both media and politicians have a responsibility to let us know later information we may have missed because we were preoccupied with something else. News should not be like a game of snap; as soon as cards of news events are laid the opportunity to comment, question and reveal is lost.

I OFTEN REFLECT on the contrast between the average Minister and civil servants when I meet them together in the corridors around parliament.

The politician, of course, swaggers badly and is loud and attention-seeking. While the civil servant always plays the church mouse. Every effort is made to conceal discreetly all trace of personality and expression. The code is to appear unexceptional. But my experience of them is that they are usually exceptional, bright and, without them, Ministers would very soon flounder.

ONE PIECE of news the Government needn't have tried to bury in my view is that of deciding no longer to give free money from the tax payer to the bottomless pit of Railtrack.[2]

The simple judgement was made that accepting Government subsidies with one hand and paying shareholders' dividends with the other, with no perceptible improvement in service, was no longer sensible politics.

The week after the Hatfield rail crash the shareholders all got massively increased dividends. The boardroom and shareholders clearly had not rewarded themselves for public service achievements.

Our rail track should be like our roads—run by the country for public and private users.

I for one am glad that this gravy train has been stopped in its tracks. My only concern is that, like far too many trains these days, it is long overdue.

16th October 2001

[1]   *Jo Moore, a special adviser to the transport and local government secretary, Stephen Byers, reportedly sent an email half an hour after the attacks on 11th September 2001, suggesting it was a good time to release difficult announcements to the media. The email produced a public outcry at Labour's obsession with spin. The email read as follows: "Alun, It's now a very good day to get out anything we want to bury. Councillors expenses? Jo."*
[2]   *On 7th October 2001 Secretary of State for Trade and Industry, Stephen Byers, succeeded in his petition to the High Court to put Railtrack plc into Administration. The action was taken following a request from the Board for additional Government funding otherwise the company would be insolvent. Mr Byers later announced that a not-for-profit company would replace Railtrack.*

Business as usual

A **GLOOM OF** futility has descended on the Commons this week. It has dawned on many that nothing MPs say or do will significantly alter the course of events. War isn't something the House customarily votes on and debates take place within the confines of acres of news coverage but limited information on what's really going on.

As Charles Kennedy's Parliamentary Private Secretary I am aware that a limited few receive more information than the rest, on "Privy Council terms". But that then limits their opportunity to speak beyond the most guarded comment which, in the end, sounds much like the generalised platitudes uttered at these times.

Those who oppose military strikes are properly asked what else they would do. But alternatives depend on knowledge of the situation in a detail not really available outside official sources.

So MPs, who like to demonstrate their clear purpose at times like these, are left looking purposeless and irrelevant; a hard pill to swallow for many of the jostling egos of the chamber of the Commons.

DESPITE THIS, quiet progress is being made…

Our campaign to abolish tuition fees for students has achieved modest success as the new Secretary of State, Estelle Morris, attempts to unpick a policy already undermined by the Liberal Democrats in the Scottish coalition.[1]

The degrading Asylum voucher system is proposed to be phased out by David Blunkett—effectively undoing much of Jack Straw's 1999 Asylum and Immigration Act.[2] Cannabis is to be downgraded as an illegal drug after Blunkett, again, was caught in possession of the idea that targeting traffickers and hard drugs was a greater priority.[3] And Government ministers have clearly softened their attitude to the promotion of privatised services.[4]

Each of these would dominate the main news for days on end, but while attention is being turned and hysteria quelled, mostly sensible and long overdue policy development is proceeding at a pace rarely seen before!

30th October 2001

[1]   *Secretary of State Rt. Hon. Estelle Morris MP announced the review in early October 2001.*
[2]   *Announced by Home Secretary Rt. Hon. David Blunkett MP on Monday 29th October 2001,*
[3]   *Ditto on Tuesday 23rd October 2001.*
[4]   *Reported on 1st October at Labour's Party Conference: "The threat of a major row over public services has been extinguished after the government pledged to review a controversial scheme under which private firms run local council services." (BBC)*

Pouring aid down wrong hole

VICTORIOUS PUNCHING of the air has not been evident in the House of Commons since news came through of the fall of Kabul and Kandahar airport.[1]

MPs, who are not normally reticent, usually save their celebrations for their own re-election. But where Afghanistan is concerned the serious job of getting aid to the now near starving people in the hills and on the borders of the country is the urgent priority.

Local people here have rightly questioned me about the military objectives of the strikes on (what we hoped were only) military and terrorist targets in Afghanistan. But generally, less attention is being given to the efforts needed to provide comfort and food to the refugees on the Pakistan and Iran border or those who are living in the hills after fleeing the cities of their country.

Some of us are now working to ensure that humanitarian aid will become a greater priority for the coalition than it has succeeded in being for the past two months.

SMALL BUSINESS men and women who rightly complain that enterprising spirit is being squeezed out of them, as they are strangled by "red tape" and regulations, will have no sympathy for MPs who are going through their annual sleaze busting scrutiny from the Parliamentary Commissioner for Standards[2]—a four day a week job which pays £76,000 a year. I suppose the Register of Members Interests makes novel reading for some although I was contacted by her office this week to be told off for giving them too much information and that they didn't want to have the level of detail I sent them.

That'll make my modest entry look conspicuously small.

PARLIAMENTARY QUESTIONS have proven this week that there is "life after death" after all!

Just when we thought public finances were safe from the black hole that is the Millennium Dome, we hear that the old corpse has cost the country £21.5 million since it closed at the beginning of the year.[3]

That's £21.5 million without even trying. This contrasts with the Herculean efforts to spend just £5 million of Objective One money in Cornwall and Scilly in the last two years.

Another Parliamentary answer seeks to reassure me that Objective One is going well and that we shouldn't be worried that local projects have only managed to claim 1.6% of the seven year budget in the first two years.[4] Perhaps the Government will recommend that we build a dome!

13th November 2001

[1]   *Kabul, capital city of Afghanistan, fell to the Northern Alliance during the night and the early morning of Monday 12th/Tuesday 13th November 2001. At the time of writing this there were also reports that the southern Afghanistan city airport of Kandahar had fallen on the same day. However, confirmation of this did not come through until Friday 7th December when Kandahar itself fell and Friday 14th December when US marines took the airport.*

[2]   *Elizabeth Filkin later decided not to apply for the job as, it was alleged, it was considered to have been "down-graded". (Reported on Tuesday 4th December 2001)*

[3]   *The Times, Monday 12th November 2001.*

[4]   *See page 183.*

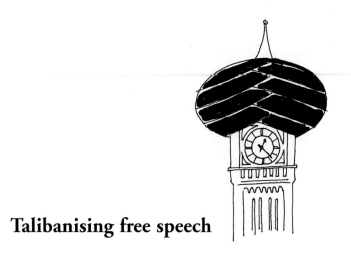

Talibanising free speech

I KNOW I SPEND a great deal of time in this column running down the deeply fallen specimens of human life—including myself, of course—found amongst the body politic. However, one thing, to the credit of our Parliament, we try not to allow is the suppression of free speech.

The strongly expressed and often polarised views of MPs are generally not censored before they are uttered. This is a good thing. Opinions which challenge cosy preconceptions and established thought aid our understanding.

The main obstacle to this is of course the operation of a Party's Whip. The disciplining of those MPs who show any sign of independent thought is something not to be witnessed by those of a nervous disposition.

But certainty amongst party rebels (or "Awkward Squad" as they're known up here) can strengthen and serious backbench revolts can be mounted. Just as it has this week when up to 21 Labour "rebels" supported Liberal Democrat amendments to the Anti Terrorism Bill which has now been rushed through Parliament.

That's why I'm sometimes surprised to find evidence in communities around the country of the "Talibanisation" of free speech. Many of those who are discouraging debate are themselves heartily cynical of the excessive use of the Whip System in politics.

On many occasions there are projects or development plans or concepts, whether in outline or detail, for which a vociferous group either strongly supports or objects.

There's nothing wrong with that, but free speech and respect for the range of views within a community must be respected if we aren't to

171

become mini replicas of the totalitarian states we all despise.

It doesn't happen on every occasion of course, but when it does it can become very uncomfortable for those who want to raise intelligent questions or who simply wish to ensure that there is an opportunity for the sober consideration of the consequences of a particular action. Or it may be necessary to seek (as I do) to ensure that where public funds are employed the public interest is protected.

Sadly, there have been occasions, even in West Cornwall, when the sweeping euphoria behind a particular campaign creates an unappetising intolerance for free speech. Anything short of manic adoration is considered heresy.

I noted in the minutes from a group planning a public meeting on a significant local matter the prior agreement that:

"anyone who attends the (public) meeting to raise objections should be asked to leave".

The possibility that those who raise serious questions or an important line of enquiry might actually improve the proposal they were seeking to support clearly hadn't crossed anyone's mind.

Those who want to have their community or country or town moving forward together shoulder to shoulder can't do that by showing the door to those who express genuine concerns.

Many of us feel superior to the authoritarian neurosis of the Taliban. But communities or countries or towns which seek to place a burka over free speech and fail to see the benefit of allowing it are destined to fail.

A climate of intolerance for other people's concerns seldom makes for a happy community under the surface; nor for successful outcomes. At some point or other the unhappiness will surface to the embarrassment of all.

27th November 2001

The arts of politics

JUST DOWN the road from Parliament it is another national institution which also becomes the focus for widespread routine derision. It certainly helps to take the heat off humble politicians.

I am of course referring to the annual "Turner Prize"[1] at the Tate Gallery about half a mile down Millbank from the Commons. Passing cabbies assume it's the annual urine extracting competition ("are they trying to take the p… or what, mate?").

I have to admit to being a pretty unreformable bumpkin on these matters, as with so many others and I do wonder whether among all the unmade beds, piles of bricks and the empty room with a light bulb going on and off, there really is some genuine artistic integrity trying to get out.

But in contrast to the lot of the oratorical artists plying their trade in The Commons it does appear that Turner Prize entrants are given generous helpings of benefit despite oceans of doubt around them. However, politicians—like benefit claimants—are assumed to be guilty until proven unfeasibly innocent.

11th December 2001

[1] The year's Turner Prize was awarded to Martin Creed on Sunday 9th December 2001 for a work entitled "Work# 227: The Lights Going on and Off".

Scatter gun of verbiage misses target

Used for target practice at Mullion school fair, 1998

PARLIAMENT HAS not yet settled back to its normal routine. Some of us have kept ourselves busy while others may still be recovering from the festivities.

Speculation over the future of the Transport Secretary, Stephen Byers, almost overshadowed a debate I had in the Commons earlier this week.[1] Because one practice which is already back to full swing, following Parliament's brief Christmas recess, is the use of the Ministerial battery of warm words, platitudes, time-wasting examples, irrelevant anecdotes and other forms of verbal "froth".

173

In this case, the Minister concerned, with 13 minutes in which to address three very simple questions, retaliated with the full artillery of avoidance tactics. The Department seems to have become so obsessed with the Railtrack administration story and speculation about the future of Mr Byers that simple questions on any other aspect of policy present too great a challenge for them.

Or perhaps it has become a tenet of macho civil servant culture that, no matter how straightforward the question, the challenge is always to turn it into a "yes-no-black-white" word game. The aim is to wear the enemy down by not addressing the subject they most want the Minister to talk about and to see if they can get to the end of a turgid brief without hesitation, deviation or repetition.

All I wanted to know was whether the Government thought that £32.4 million of subsidy to Scottish Island Ferry services when the Isles of Scilly got nothing was acceptable or not; whether her department had a view on the staggeringly awful rail service Cornwall has endured for the past two years; and whether they thought it was a good idea that the Cornish rail service would be cut off at the Tamar over the busy Easter weekend or not.

It was only an intervention on my part which stopped the Minister filling all the time available by telling the House "what a wonderful 10 year transport strategy they had and how either 'this' method or 'that' approach might help rural bus services but we'll have to wait and see and so on" and forced her to at least attempt the beginnings of an answer.

In the corridors after the debate when speaking to the Minister "off the record" I found that she could have given me some pretty straightforward and helpful answers.

"So why didn't you say that in the debate!?" quoth I.

"Ah well,…" I was hit by another volley of verbal sedative.

However, one thing we could all agree on throughout the Commons was our deep condolences for Chancellor Gordon Brown and his wife at the loss of their 10 day old daughter. We privately send our thoughts and prayers to them and hope that they'll be given solace from public and media intrusion at this very difficult time.

8th January 2002

[1] *Commons debate led by Andrew George MP "Rural and Island Transport" on 8th January 2002.*

Respite for prisoners of war

MANY CONSIDER that it brings shame on western nations. They were led from their cages, hooded, gagged and shackled. United Nations' Conventions on detention and torture had clearly been flouted.

But, you know, in spite of the clear evidence, many of my Parliamentary colleagues and I did not believe it was fair that Government Whips continued to treat their own backbenchers in this manner.

Those who had been permitted to speak up for themselves compared their handling with the relative molly coddling of suspected Al Q'aeda terrorists in Cuba this week.[1] One, shaking with terror, even claimed that he'd been threatened with a bowl of pretzels.[2]

My Liberal Democrat colleagues and I clearly thought that this was a situation which was rapidly getting out of hand and so launched into a series of headlong assaults on the Government front line.

One in particular involved a gladiatorial battle over the Government policy on care and residential care homes. A great deal of effort went into the job of attempting to knock chunks out of each other and which shed only heat rather than light on an important matter on which an impending crisis is looming. Many of us, who had been looking forward to a considered debate, sat in gloom at the prospect of a pointless battle leading to an unappetising stalemate.

The ritual of point scoring across the chamber is deeply unedifying if you discover that the basis of your concerns is used as convenient ammunition to lob at your opponent.

But at least it takes the Government's eyes off the activities of the Lobby fodder behind them and provides an opportunity for light relief.

22nd January 2002

[1]   On the 11 January 2002 the first Al Q'aeda prisoners were flown into Guantanamo Bay (The Times 11/01/02). Media attention quickly focused on the alleged flouting of human rights conventions and reported inhumane treatment of "chained and shackled" prisoners whom the US failed to name "prisoners of war".
[2]   On 13 January 2002 President Bush, watching the Superbowl on TV in the Whitehouse choked on a salty pretzel snack, fainted and fell off his couch, causing a conspicuous red bruise to his cheek.

Cast adrift in the sea of uncertainty

PERHAPS WE GOT our priorities wrong.
The country has been gripped with anxiety about whether Will or Gareth would secure poll position as "pop idol".[1] Meanwhile politicians have been occupying their time with relatively trivial matters, like tackling the "axis of evil"[2] across the world and dealing with the "wreckers"[3] of civilization as we know it.

This may all sound a bit trifling in comparison with selecting pop idols, but grey and dull politicians have this habit of failing to reflect the real concerns of people in this modern age.

And just to make matters worse, there was the Prime Minister leaving the whole country in the lurch by popping off to Africa for a few days.

A bandwagon—clearly destined to go nowhere—was got up from the Tory benches, convinced that the whole country would go to the dogs whilst the PM was away. How would we cope? Panic set in.

The leaders behind this campaign were convinced that unless Tony Blair himself was present to oversee personally all NHS operations, commuter trains, etc., then the country would surely collapse, followed by the certain end of civilization.

Well, the PM came back and I don't think anything happened which might demand the immediate confiscation of his passport.

While he was away, I don't know whether Tony Blair crossed President Bush's defined "axis of evil"[4] but, if he did, I doubt he recognised it.

Closer to home, my office is beginning to feel the strain of public concern over the future of West Cornwall Hospital.[5]

Already the "spin" and "language bending" has commenced and the consultation document isn't out until 4th March.

We already know that we will be reassured that the review team has considered and consulted more than throughout the whole history of mankind and that the process has been so open that we all know the contents of their minds before they do.

If we disagree we will be told that it is the people of West Cornwall rather than hospital chiefs who are "resistant to change".

We know it's a David and Goliath battle in which all of the cards are stacked against us, but we will fight for investment in emergency admissions at the Penzance site because we know it's right.

But I'm sure we won't describe those we disagree with as existing in an "axis of evil"!

The truth about the debate on a small hospital, as much as about international relations, is that we are all often floundering in a sea of uncertainty. There is no obviously safe land of "good" nor hard rocks of "evil"!

We must consider what's best for West Cornwall, but for the review managers to prove convincingly that they are "open", the team will have to demonstrate an open mind, accept that their plans could put patients in greater danger and show that they are prepared to be flexible.

12th February 2002

[1]   *Pop Idol 2002 was the UK's most successful live entertainment show ever. Starting in October 2001 with 5.6 million viewers, millions flocked to the show, over 14 million watched the showdown finale between Gareth and Will, 8.6 million called to vote and nearly 13 million came back to ITV to see the tears flow when the result was announced that Will had won on 9th February 2002.*
[2]   *President Bush's State of the Union address, 29/01/02 (CNN) "The Iraqi regime is a regime that has something to hide from the civilized world…States like these, and their terrorist allies, constitute an axis of evil, arming to threaten the peace of the world. They could attack our allies or attempt to blackmail the United States. In any of these cases, the price of indifference would be catastrophic."*
[3]   *Tony Blair, Labour Party Conference 03/02/02 (BBC News) "[The Tories]…can only ever begin to make the political case for [spending cuts] if they run the public services down. Our strategy is to build up the public services. Theirs is to knock them down. Reformers versus wreckers. That is the battle for this parliament and it is one we must win." There was some speculation that the reference 'wreckers' was also a coded criticism of Trade Unions at a time when relationships with No.10 were already becoming strained.*
[4]   *See footnote 2. The countries named in the 'axis of evil' address were Somalia, North Korea, Iran, Iraq.*
[5]   *After nearly two years of review local health trusts have proposed that the 81-bed acute hospital no longer take any/many emergency admissions. The three month public consultation was due to close at the end of May 2002.*

More spun against than spinning

THE CORNISH are of course resigned to being regularly duffed up by the metropolitan elite for being helplessly insular and dreadfully parochial…though quaint!

But, you know, the more I see of the London crowd the less I'm prepared to accept criticism from them.

With the continuing crisis in health, the prospect of tax increases, the failed challenges of meeting recycling targets or energy from renewable sources, the legacy of the failed privatisation of rail still to be properly dealt with and the challenge of brokering peace in the Middle East before the Israeli/Palestinian conflict destabilises the rest of the world, surely there is enough political meat there for thoughtful urbane journalists to get their teeth into. But no.

The Westminster media pack have got easier meat; stirring up a minor soap opera by picking at the entrails of a few office memos.

Having scented blood, the pack are pursuing their favourite quarry. The sport of Minister baiting is in full swing. Nothing short of an abject resignation will satisfy the baying hounds.[1]

Opposition politicians cannot believe their luck as they are led from the torpor of the substitutes bench to be presented with an open goal. Needless to say, it would be churlish to do anything other than to slam the ball into the back of the net with the fullest vigour. With no one to trip them up, and being egged on by the press who set up the opportunity for them, they naturally demand immediate resignations.

Though the chattering classes of the Westminster village are frothing with excitement as a minor sub plot has made headline news for over ten days, most well-balanced folk consider whatever Byers said to Sixsmith or vice-versa with monumental indifference.

I had discussed a number of pressing political issues with Liberal Democrat Leader Charles Kennedy at the weekend prior to a couple of prime time radio interviews. While we had agreed that tax, the economy, transport and health were amongst the most important matters, interviewers dismissed these as minor affairs as they worked themselves into a lather of almost indecent excitement about the Byers "Spingate" story.

Bewildered, all we could do was to watch helplessly as the "on the hour" news contorted Charles's relatively cautious comments into blood-curdling headline news.

The absurdity of it all does not stop there. Not one iota of this nonsense has helped late train services become more punctual. None of the hours of broadcast and forests of newsprint have improved government policy.

All it has done is to feed the self-serving frenzy of Westminster village spin-doctors and media pundits who really ought to get out a bit more.

IN CONTRAST last week I attended the launch of an impressive new train which we hope will provide a more punctual service for Virgin than we have been used to.

I am sorry to say that (even with my relatively limited knowledge of the Cornish language) I was the first to point out the misspelling of the Cornish name which had just been unveiled—Vyajer Kernewek (Cornish Voyager).

Even amongst the warring factions of devotees of different spelling systems of the Cornish language no-one would agree that you could spell Kernewek without the 'n'.

Needless to say, faces which became as red as the Virgin logo, betrayed that this was a mistake and not done deliberately. I felt sorrow rather than anger. Immediate resignations were not demanded and I hope the costly error can soon be put right.

In what was a lesson in thorough double-checking, we all knew that this could so easily happen to any one of us.

The error spelt embarrassment for some but, like the train, we have to move on.

26th February 2002

(181) (1) In that week up to the 2 March 2002, the Moore/Sixsmith/Byers memo saga registered 2431 column inches in the national press, more than any other story (The Editor Magazine, a Guardian supplement published 2/3/02). The internal dispute resulted in the resignations or sackings (depending on version) of Martin Sixsmith and Jo Moore.

APPENDIX

PAGE 30

[2] Mr. Andrew George (St. Ives): *Does the Prime Minister agree that the Multilateral Agreement on Investment (MAI), if resurrected by the World Trade Organisation, would be nothing more than a solution without a problem? Does he believe that his friend in France, Mr Jospin, was right or wrong to withdraw French Government support from the MAI?*

The Prime Minister: *We have made it clear that we support achieving agreement. I do not agree with the Hon. Gentleman that the MAI is a solution without a problem. All these measures are part of trying to break down barriers to trade between countries. This country is a trading nation, and it is in our interest to have trade that is as free and open as possible. I would have thought that that was in the best traditions of the Liberal Party.* **Hansard, 4th November 1998.**

PAGE 31

[3] *I was wrong. General Pinochet eventually returned to Chile in March 2000 after the Home Secretary, Jack Straw, decided that Pinochet was unfit for extradition to Spain to stand trial for crimes committed by his regime. The saga began in October 1998 when Pinochet was arrested while recovering from a back operation in a London hospital. The week before he had taken tea with Baroness (Margaret) Thatcher, who defended the General throughout his time in Britain.*

PAGE 82

[2] Mr. Andrew George (St Ives): *If achieving social and economic inclusion is the biggest challenge a Government can set themselves, what decisive action will the Prime Minister take to guarantee the efficient and effective delivery of public-matched funds to the poorest regions of the United Kingdom, namely European Union Objective One regions?*

The Prime Minister: *We are looking at how we can make the proper arrangements for the co-ordination of matched funding. Under the new procedures and the new deal that we secured, 75 per cent of the money for Objective One comes from the European Union. That is a big increase on the previous position. As a result of Objective One status being given to Cornwall, which is the area represented by the Hon. Gentleman and others, it will receive some £320 million during the next seven years.*
(3rd November 1999, Column 292)

PAGE 92

[1]   Michael White, Political Editor, The Guardian, Thursday 27th January 2000.
   "Tony Blair's 1,000th day in power was last night marked by squabbling and parliamentary spoiling tactics by MPs after hardline Unionist and Tory critics of the Good Friday agreement talked through the night and most of yesterday—wrecking William Hague's plans to nail the Prime Minister at Question Time.

   The outburst of old-fashioned guerrilla tactics in the Commons, which caught both front-benches off guard, prompted a bizarre exchange of faxed letters between the two party leaders in which Mr Hague, in effect, asked Mr Blair to use his 178-seat Commons majority to stop the Tory Unionist filibuster. It was the first time since 1986 that the ritual exchange, held every Wednesday at 3 pm, had been lost because the previous day's business had not ended in time. The last time a full day's Commons business was lost in this way was in 1988.

   Though the Shadow Home Secretary Ann Widdecombe had promised a 'fair passage' to the brief bill as recently as Monday—and did not oppose its second reading that day—Unionists like Willie Ross MP and the maverick Tory right winger, Eric Forth, a formidable backbench operator, led a filibuster against the clause-by-clause examination that started on Tuesday afternoon."

PAGE 113

[3]   Mr. Andrew George (St. Ives):   If he will visit West Cornwall and the Isles of Scilly   in the St. Ives constituency.
The Prime Minister: I am sorry to say that I have no immediate plans to do so.
Mr. George: That is a pity because, as I am sure the Prime Minister knows Cornwall has a distinctive culture and identity that allows it to play a full part in the celebration of diversity here and in the wider world. Has he heard yesterday's truly shocking news from Marazion in my constituency? It is alleged that a group of youths abused, physically and racially, a visiting party of young people from Berlin. Does the Prime Minister agree that, if certain members of the political elite in the Chamber abuse their privilege by appealing to base instincts and artfully blaming asylum seekers, blaming Europe and blaming foreigners at every opportunity, it is little wonder that we find in Marazion, as elsewhere, that we reap what we sow.
The Prime Minister: I agree entirely. Of course, we condemn that attack and detest xenophobic racism of any sort. We are glad and proud to be a country that welcomes people from abroad and engages in proper cultural ties with other countries. I hope that we all welcome that.
Prime Ministers Questions, House of Commons, 7th June 2000 (column 287)

PAGE 129

[3]   The US Presidential election of 7th November 2000 produced the closest ever result. Despite Democrat Al Gore winning the popular vote, the Republican candidate George W Bush was declared to have won the Electoral College, which came down to

a disputed handful of votes in the State of Florida. After court challenges and recounts Al Gore conceded the Presidency on 14th December 2000. Bush was sworn in as President on 20th January 2001. Figures published in late 2001 indicated that Gore had actually won Florida and consequently, both the popular vote and the Electoral College, and that he should therefore have become the 43rd President in Bush's place. Will Hutton wrote in The Observer on Sunday 24th December 2000, "I never thought I would live to see it. There has been a right-wing coup in the United States. It is now clear beyond any doubt that the winner of the Presidential election was Al Gore. In Florida the votes are being counted unofficially in a way the Supreme Court would not permit: he was already 140 votes ahead when counting stopped for Christmas and his final lead promises to be in the thousands. Nationally he leads by over half a million votes. What has happened is beyond outrage. It is the cynical misuse of power by a conservative elite nakedly to serve its interests—and all of us should be frightened for the consequences."

PAGE 170

Structural Funding

Andrew George: *To ask the Secretary of State for Trade and Industry what (a) amount and (b) proportion of overall EU objective 1 budget for the UK has been (i) committed and (ii) spent according to the latest records in each of the four objective 1 regions. [14452]*
Alan Johnson: *The figures in the table are the latest available commitments and payments made under the EU structural funds for each of the objective 1 regions. Payments under the programmes lag behind commitments because the fund regulations require ERDF expenditure to be defrayed before it is claimed. ESF projects may receive an advance payment at the beginning of the project but subsequent ESF payments take place after expenditure has been defrayed.*
The management of the objective 1 programme for West Wales and the Valleys is a matter for the National Assembly for Wales. However, I understand from the National Assembly that the figures for this region are as set out in the table.

Region	Committed grant (£ million)	Spent grant (£ million)	Proportion of regional objective 1 budget (Percentage)
Cornwall and the Scilly Isles	60	5.98	19.53/1.95
Merseyside	64.73	30.68	20.14/3.75
South Yorkshire	92.5	13.046	12.86/1.81
West Wales and the Valleys	260	30.4	24/2.7

183

INDEX

ON 2ND MAY 1997 Andrew George became Liberal Democrat MP for the St Ives Constituency of West Cornwall and the Isles of Scilly. In 2001 he increased his majority from 7,170 to over 10,000.

Born in Mullion on the Lizard peninsula in 1958, Andrew went to schools in Mullion, Cury and Helston; then Sussex and Oxford Universities, graduating with an MSc in Agricultural Economics. After years away in what he calls "England", Andrew returned to work for the Cornwall Rural Community Council. He stood for Parliament in 1992 and slashed the sitting Tory MP's majority from 8,000 to 1,600.

He is committed to Cornwall. He was the first to use Cornish in the House of Commons, where he has served on the Agriculture Select Committee and is Shadow Fisheries Minister. He is Parliamentary Private Secretary to the Liberal Democrat Leader, the Rt Hon Charles Kennedy MP.

He is Chair, Vice Chair or Secretary of several All Party Parliamentary groups; campaigns for fishermen, farmers, victims of domestic violence, disability, housing, health services, third world interests and economic development; helped establish the Council for Racial Equality in Cornwall (of which he is President) and is a Trustee of the Rural Race Equality Action Project.

He is also proud to be President of the West Cornwall Reliant Robin Owners' Club. Sadly he is not fortunate to own one himself.

Andrew and his St Ives-born wife Jill live in Hayle with their daughter Morvah and Davy, their son.

Andrew George plays football, cricket and rugby with various local and Parliamentary teams; swims, cycles and enjoys most sports except hunting with dogs.